MANAGEMENT BY CONSCIOUSNESS

MANAGEMENT
BY CONSCIOUSNESS

A Spirituo-technical Approach

EDITED BY
DR. G. P. GUPTA

SRI AUROBINDO INSTITUTE
OF RESEARCH IN SOCIAL SCIENCES
SRI AUROBINDO SOCIETY
PONDICHERRY - 605 002

First Edition: 1994
Reprinted: 1996, 1998, 2004, 2009

Rs. 120.00
ISBN 978-81-7060-080-0

Published by Sri Aurobindo Institute of
Research in Social Sciences, a unit of
Sri Aurobindo Society, Pondicherry - 605 002
Website: www.sriaurobindosociety.org.in
Printed at Sri Aurobindo Ashram Press, Pondicherry

Printed in India

Contents

APPENDICES

PREFACE

Management, as it obtains today, is a discipline borrowed from the West, especially the USA. This has reduced 'man' to a mere worker engaged always in the stream of economic order – he is a cog in the huge machinery of production and distribution. Consequently, the material progress has been the index of growth, development and prosperity.

Management has thus remained to be a lever of materialism keeping apart the consciousness aspect of men and materials. Whereas the man has received all material considerations, his integrality of character and personality has been set apart from his work and his working conditions. Rather, the person, as labourer, has become an objectified and standardised component of the production process. This view of 'labourer' has tended to divorce man as a social and spiritual being from his 'productive' role at work. This has reaffirmed the lingering lesson of the centuries that one's spiritual and social life should reside outside the work-place. The hard fact is that a man is a bundle of so many ingredients – physical, vital, mental, psychic and spiritual and he responds quickly and readily if these components are touched upon and developed.

With a view to unfolding this aspect of management, this anthology has been prepared by jotting down articles by reputed authors on the subject. The Editor is indeed very grateful to the authors for their contributions. Also, he is thankful to the publishers of these articles to which due acknowledgement is recorded herein.

At the end are given a few Appendices which pinpoint some of the basic issues appearing in the management process. Although these issues have also figured in the textual discussions their treatment was only contextual and cursory. The Appendices present an exhaustive treatment of the basic issues involved.

The Editor will feel amply rewarded if the Anthology will touch upon and motivate all those engaged in the practice of management towards considering MAN in his integral personality and thus moulding their management techniques and philosophy on 'consciousness approach' which is basic to man and management and is the core of Indian Heritage.

EDITOR

THE WAY-OUT

'Mankind has long been experimenting with various kinds of thought, different principles of ethics, strange dreams of a perfection to be gained by material means, impossible millenniums and humanitarian hopes. Nowhere has it succeeded in realising the ultimate secret of life. Nowhere has it found satisfaction. No scheme of society or politics has helped it to escape from the necessity of sorrow, poverty, strife, dissatisfaction from which it strives for an outlet; for whoever is trying to find one by material means must inevitably fail.... But the grand workshop of spiritual experiment, the laboratory of the soul has been India, where thousands of great spirits have been born in every generation who were content to work quietly in their own souls, perfect their knowledge, hand down the results of their experiments to a few disciples and leave the rest to others to complete... the work which we have to do for humanity is a work which no other nation can accomplish – the spiritualisation of the race....'

SRI AUROBINDO
(*SABCL, Vol. 1, p. 799*)

ACKNOWLEDGEMENT

The Editor expresses his profound gratitude and acknowledges with thanks to Sri Aurobindo Ashram Trust, Pondicherry for having included in the anthology the articles on 'Consciousness Approach to Business Management' (authored by Mr. Gary Jacobs) and 'The Mother's Ministry of Management' (authored by the Editor himself) published in the *Mother India* – Monthly Review of Culture edited by Shri K. D. Sethna and published by the Trust.

Also have been excerpted and reproduced partially the words and writings by Sri Aurobindo and the Mother from their Centenary Volumes released and copy-righted by the Ashram Trust. To these, too, the Editor gratefully mentions his acknowledgement to the publishers. Titles to the writings of Sri Aurobindo and the Mother have been given by the Editor.

Some of the writings or parts thereof, included in the anthology, had also been previously published in *The Span*, New Delhi, *The Indian Heritage*, Madras, *The Economic Times*, Bombay, *The Indian Management*, Delhi and *The World Union, Mother India, The Advent,* Pondicherry. Our thankful acknowledgement to their editors and publishers.

BUSINESS AND SPIRITUALITY

...I do not regard business as something evil or tainted, any more than it is so regarded in ancient spiritual India. If I did, I would not be able to receive money from X or from those of our disciples who in Bombay trade with East Africa; nor could we then encourage them to go on with their work but would have to tell them to throw it up and attend to their spiritual progress alone. How are we to reconcile X's seeking after spiritual light and his mill? Ought I not to tell him to leave his mill to itself and to the devil and go into some Ashram to meditate? Even if I myself had had the command to do business as I had the command to do politics I would have done it without the least spiritual or moral compunction. All depends on the spirit in which a thing is done, the principles on which it is built and the use to which it is turned. I have done politics and the most violent kind of revolutionary politics, *ghoram karma*, and I have supported war and sent men to it, even though politics is not always or often a very clean occupation nor can war be called a spiritual line of action. But Krishna calls upon Arjuna to carry on war of the most terrible kind and by his example encourage men to do every kind of human work, *sarva-karmāṇi*. Do you contend that Krishna was an unspiritual man and that his advice to Arjuna was mistaken or wrong in principle? Krishna goes further and declares that a man by doing in the right way and in the right spirit the work dictated to him by his fundamental nature, temperament and capacity and according to his and its *dharma* can move towards the Divine. He validates the function and *dharma* of the Vaishya as well as of the Brahmin and Kshatriya. It is in his view quite possible for a man to do business and make money and earn profits and yet be a spiritual man, practise yoga, have an inner life. The Gita is constantly justifying works as a means of spiritual salvation and enjoining a Yoga of Works as well as of Bhakti and Knowledge. Krishna, however, superimposes a higher law also that work must be done without desire, without attachment to any fruit or reward, without any egoistic attitude or motive, as an offering or sacrifice to the Divine. This is the traditional Indian attitude towards these things, that all work can be done if it is done according to the *dharma* and, if it is rightly done, it does not prevent the approach to the Divine or the access to spiritual knowledge and the spiritual life.

SRI AUROBINDO
(*SABCL, Vol. 23, pp. 675-76*)

1

MANAGEMENT WITH A DIFFERENCE

Charity begins at home. Likewise, management begins from Man. On being asked as to what he actually produced, built or manufactured, the President of a giant multinational corporation replies quietly: "I do not manufacture automobiles nor do I prepare shoe-strings; I build only men because my men build these things."

This frank admission by the corporation President speaks volumes on the role and significance of MAN in a scheme of management programme. In any work-system, may be home, hotel, hospital, business, industry or State, management enters into through its various ramifications: management of time and jobs, means and methods, money and material, men and machinery, plans and priorities, policies and practice.

Harmony

Management is thus an orderly conduct of activities in any field of human endeavour. Management is to strike harmony in working – a balance and equilibrium in thoughts and actions, goals and achievements, plans, procedures and performance, products and markets. To put it differently, management means computation of the gone-by, care of the current and caution for the future. It casts an all-pervading effect. In real terms, the urgency of management seeks to resolve situations of scarcities. Maximisation of results with minimisation of resources through better allocation and utilization process, is perhaps the test of a better management system.

Notice a herd of cattle moving homeward at the end of the day: all in a group returning leisurely with perfect faithful following – but in what a disorder and disarray blocking the broad highway to fast-moving motorists, ministers and managers, calling them to halt and causing them detention and delay in catching their flight-schedules or missing their public meetings. They move on but in disarray, they reach home but with delay and detentions. They have no regulation, no discipline and perhaps no demands. Time is not the essence of matter to them. In contrast, imagine an infantry column of an army-unit: ranks and files in order of size/seniority, well-formed rows, harmony in movement and speed, command and discipline and no waste of time or energy either of themselves or of the motorists, ministers or pedestrians. The difference is obvious. Here enters the role of discipline and consciousness. Automaticity is the essence of the matter. In management, that manager is the best who manages the least.

The negation of management is disorder, confusion, wastage, detention, delay, decadence and death. Why? Just recall a dinner-programme you are invited to with your family and friends. The number of invitees is not very large – all friends and familiar faces. The stocks are there in plenty, the tables are well-set and the menu is also well-arranged. But alas! the mode of replenishment on the serving tables is poor and flimsy. Obviously, quite a few invitees have to return disappointed and insatiated. Spontaneously, one calls the event as 'poor organisation'. The stocks were there but the mode was faulty – the system was lacking – and, all-told, there was mismanagement. Some would brand it as 'utter confusion.' See what Sri Aurobindo, in one of his letters, advises:

> Orderly harmony and organisation in physical things is a necessary part of efficiency and perfection and makes the instrument fit for whatever work is given to it.... In the most physical things you have to fix a programme in order to deal with them, otherwise all becomes a sea of confusion and haphazard. Fixed rules have also to be made for the management of material things so long as people are not sufficiently developed to deal with them in the right way without rules.
>
> Rules are indispensable for the orderly management of work, for without order and arrangement nothing can be properly done, all becomes clash, confusion and disorder.

Consciousness

Management presupposes the existence of man. No man, no management. Man is the first syllable in MANagement. Management has been in vogue with the appearance of man on this planet. Even when man was in a wild state of his uncivilised living – an aboriginal in himself – he must have felt the need of managing for himself a hunt for his hunger and shelter for living. It was his needs, urge and efforts that he had to set out in search of food and shelter. That was the beginning of managing for the self. He must have felt, thought, planned, moved, exerted and finally procured something for his survival and development. And by the process of trial and error he could manage for more and better. And this process has been a continuous and ceaseless human endeavour towards discovering more and more, better and still better by planning and perseverance till we have now arrived at the most sophisticated means and tools of management, discovery of robots and a systematic philosophy of management science. However, the basic element behind this life-pattern remains to be Man. Management must therefore be taken to be an effort of man, for man and for humanity.

Now, as it obtains today, management has become a need for an orderly and progressive life. With growth and development of science and technology economic activities and programmes have multiplied beyond size and imagination. Trade has expanded beyond limits, industry has grown beyond dimensions. The world (Universe?) has become too small to travel. Was it not an achievement of management technology to have planned for pitching base-camps in the Himalayas, regularising supplies and forging human unity and team-work to have reached the highest top of the earth – to scale the Everest? Was it not again a feat of management to have set foot – not once – on the surface of the erstwhile mythological Moon? A wonderful feat of managing men, methods and resources! And will it not be another feat of management (not in distant future) to exploit and extract wealth from the fathomless ocean and deep-rooted bosom of the Earth?

As a sequel to modern management, the world has become too small to go about. We have already entered into the age of robots and computers when, perhaps, human mind and hands are sought to be done away with. Production has become automatic and in plenty. As of today, man does not grow and produce to satisfy the existing demands – he goes on producing in anticipation of demand. Also, he does not produce or manufacture to himself, his family, his neighbours, his countrymen – he produces for the humanity he knows not, converses not and perhaps imagines not. Production goes on incessantly irrespective of demand and demand is created in anticipation of products in the making. Production and distribution have become independent feats of modern industrialism. Management which was once a personal and direct action has now become an indirect feat and phenomenon. 'Produce or perish' is the call of modern industrialism.

Western Approach

This change in the management thought has brought in its train a lure for materialism – more and more goods, still better goods, variety of goods and also, cheaper goods irrespective of cost, quality and service. And this race for production and distribution has brought forth a lust for profit all round. Ends rule supreme, means are discounted. Management, therefore, has been reduced to be the handmaid of profiteering. This phenomenon is found in abundance in the West – especially the USA which has become the leader of the world both in materialism and management. Management by materialism has won fancy of poor and developing countries of the world. India makes no exception to this. Although

India has entered upon modern industrialism only recently she has relied for management technology essentially on the West. And this pattern of management naturally rests upon giant-like industries, massive and round-the-clock production and productivity of the worker.

The Western approach of management has placed utmost reliance on man, the worker. The core of Western thought is the worker – an efficient workman, a skilful worker and a productive member of the work-force. All their plans and efforts veer round the development of a productive worker – an efficient workman. They pay more so that the worker may work more and better, they reward and reimburse him so that he remains locked up with them as a lever of contributing profits. All higher salaries and heavy pay-packets, rewards and remunerations, housing facilities, recreation devices, participative programmes and other welfare schemes are directed either to meet the requirements of industrial enactments or merely to aim at enhancing, for the time being, the proficiency of the work-force so that more and better work may be extracted from the worker. This has given rise to indirect form of management. Management and workers have become different entities – their appoach is different, their interests are diverse and their claims are conflicting. The management wants to pay as little as possible for more and more work and output. In contrast, the work-force aim at working as little as possible for as much, in terms of wages and benefits, as may be extracted. There has remained no more common approach and understanding between workers and managers. Their slogan is joint-venture but their interests and actions are diverse, differing and conflicting.

Soulless Management

To the western management the worker is all, MAN stands nowhere. He is treated like a hired commodity which is paid for and rewarded as long as it is service-able. The moment he ceases to be such he stands discarded and is promptly replaced. The work-force, too, resort to underhand pressures just to extract as much as possible to dupe the management. Conflicts are common, violence is rampant, absenteeism is the rule and strikes and break-downs are daily occurrences. Naturally, production is lost, unemployment emerges and society suffers. The materialistic management has, therefore, done more harm than good. The capitalist has grown richer, man has been reduced to a hired wage-earner and society has been placed, for quantity, quality and price of goods, to the mercy of the materia-list-management. The management, not infrequently, complains against the non-cooperative outlook and attitude of the workers, despite fat salaries, heavy pay-packets and sundry real benefits. On the other side, the workers, more often than not, feel aggrieved against their pay-masters for having reduced them as their puppets. Both blame each other. There is no sense of belonging, no co-operative organisation, no fellow-feelings and the least common approach and designs.

One obvious result of this pernicious form of western management system has been the disregard of human approach, loss of human values and the erosion of human touch in the organisational hierarchy. The crisis of confidence prevails in both camps. To cut short, the western management although acquired prosperity to some for some time has absolutely failed in their aim to ensure human betterment and social welfare. The society has suffered and deteriorated, the worker has remained demoralised, the consumer has been by-passed and man has suffered loss of dignity and his due. The management too is not a nett gainer. He has earned millions but only at the cost of his sound sleep. He suffers from insomnia, gastric complaints, high blood-pressure, heart-ailments and mental discomforts. He fattens his coffers but suffers from mental unrest. Labour troubles, production losses, erosion of markets, tax measures and reduction of profits haunt his mind yielding only sleeplessness and then resort to the sleeping pills. Wealth is gained but soul is lost. Let us quote here the warning by Sri Aurobindo:

> Do not dream that when thou hast got rid of material poverty, men will ever so be happy or satisfied or society freed from ills, troubles and problems. This is only the first and lowest necessity. While the soul within remains defectively organised there will always be outward unrest, disorder and revolution.*

No wonder, therefore, that the materialist management of the Western style has remained only to be a 'soulless management.'

* *The Hour of God* (Cent. Ed. Vol. 17), p. 103.

Fresh Thinking

It becomes imperative, therefore, that fresh thinking is done on objectives, scope and contents of the management discipline. In the changed context of individual claims for self-development and social responsibility, management thought needs be re-written and re-defined so as to underline the development of Man in contrast to mere development of a wage-earner. Any worker, whatever category he may belong to, is first a MAN and then a WORKER. His needs and demands, as a human being, are more important than his claims as a wage-earner. His needs as a man are not merely his physical needs of food and shelter and even his needs and aspirations as a member of a group or a family. A man is not merely a mass of flesh, blood and bones, not even a precarious amalgam of hands and feet. A worker, as a man, is also a bundle of feelings, emotions, sentiments, likes and dislikes, priorities and preferences. He has his physique, his vital, mind, heart, spirit and soul. He is an awakened entity with consciousness. His conscience speaks, his soul guides. He undoubtedly lives on the satisfaction of his bodily needs but he grows and survives on food for his soul. He has to be contented for his physical needs, satiated for his mental demands but satisfied for his needs and demands of the soul. To quote Sri Aurobindo again:

> Man has not been seen by the thought of India as a living body developed by physical Nature which has evolved certain vital propensities, an ego, a mind and a reason, an animal of the *genus homo* and

in our case of the species *homo indicus*, whose life and education must be turned towards a satisfaction of these propensities under the government of a trained mind and reason and for the best advantage of the personal and the national ego... nor to regard man pre-eminently as a reasoning animal – a thinking, feeling and willing natural existence, a mental son of physical Nature... or as a political, social and economic being. All these are no doubt aspects of a human being... but they are outward things, parts of the instrumentation of his mind, life and action, not the whole or the real man.

India has seen always in man the individual a soul, a portion of the Divinity enwrapped in mind and body, a conscious manifestation in Nature of the universal self and spirit. Always she has distinguished and cultivated in him a mental, an intellectual, an ethical, dynamic and practical, aesthetic and hedonistic, a vital and physical being, but all these have been seen as powers of the soul that manifests through them and grows with their growth.

Man is thus an integrated creation of the Divine Craftsman. His MAN is more important than our worker – a hired wage-earner. There is nothing like an 'hierarchy of needs' as claimed by Western Thought – all needs go together and simultaneously – all needs are parallelly and equally important.

Incentives are important for motivating people towards better work. But a worker has also to be satisfied for his soul. Managers must ponder over such steps as justice and fairness in thoughts and actions, sincerity of purpose and words, awakening of consciousness, feelings of patriotism and nationalism, spontaneity of actions, aesthetic values, creation and satisfaction of higher aspirations, promotion of good-will and oneness, behavioural decencies, satisfaction of religious and moral aspirations, human touch, sense of spirituality through instructional and behavioural programmes and organisational adjustments.

Developmental Process

In the changed social order management ceases to be a career-discipline; it is for all practical purposes a developmental process. Man has to be dressed up and developed in an integrated form and size. A good man, a satisfied man, a noble man, and a co-operative man with national outlook, cultural contents and leadership qualities develops into a good and responsible worker, and not that a good worker and an effecient workman makes a good Man. The management approach has to be focussed upon development of man and not merely to train and retrain a worker. A worker has to be made soul-conscious – that he is guided by his soul to serve the Divine through his work and behaviour. Is it not true that work through human body is the best prayer to the Divine? The management should do all that helps the worker to develop his physique, broaden his outlook, energise his mental faculties, grow his consciousness and enrich his soul. Human development in an organisation should be the aim of management programmes. Man, as such, is an imperfect being – his mind is only an instrument of thought and not a fountain of knowledge. Knowledge emerges from conscience and soul. Hence soul should be suitably developed in order to make man responsive. Sincerity should be his principal tool of action. Management can do so not by mere words but by actions. Man, by nature is imitative – he begins doing what he actually sees and observes. Seeing is Believing. Management should, therefore, be action-oriented. They should do what they want to be done:

> One must not treat human nature like a machine to be handled according to rigid mental rules – a great plasticity is needed in dealing with its complex motives.

Instances are not lacking when with all the high wages, real benefits, training and re-training programmes, welfare schemes, educational instructions, management concepts of efficiency and productivity, workers, as soon as they mix with a group of hostiles, turn affront against all principles and ideals of work and decency and have indulged into all kinds of baser activities against authorities and have thrown the whole social fabric in jeopardy. Why? Because their soul was not touched and tended; their conscience was not positively nurtured and because their aspect of Man was not suitably developed and enriched. The substance is: a good man with a noble heart and soul shall make a good and a responsible worker, although the opposite may not be true.

Observe what Sri Aurobindo lays down on this aspect of Man and Management:

For man intellectually developed, mighty in scientific knowledge and mastery of gross and subtle nature, using the elements as his servants and the world as his footstool, but undeveloped in heart and spirit, becomes only an inferior kind of *asura* using the powers of a demigod to satisfy the nature of an animal.

He goes on to say:

A cultivated eye without a cultivated spirit makes by no means the highest type of man.

Tennyson had also described him 'as an eye well practised in Nature, a spirit bounded and poor.'

Management has thus to rely on the development of heart and soul. It should be 'management by soul', 'management by consciousness'. The consciousness of the worker and also of the management has to be transformed towards social commitment and new social order. Management will sustain when it succeeds in creating self-discipline among all those working in an organisation. The West has amplified on 'management by objectives', 'management by results' and 'management by performance'. But the hub of all these is the MAN – he should be developed, his soul must be enriched and activated. This alone will make a universal Truth that will never fail.

Dr. G. P. Gupta

2

THE YOGIC APPROACH TO MANAGEMENT

During the last few years, we have been bandying certain words – planning, productivity, management, not to mention democracy, socialism, secularism – and the words are being used almost promiscuously, as if we can indeed make them mean just what we, for the nonce, want them to mean. We are all for economic growth. And growth calls for productivity. And productivity is encompassed by good 'management'. Almost twenty years ago, the noted economist Dr. P.S. Lokanathan declared: "If any single factor is the key for unlocking the force of economic growth, that factor is management." He exhorted universities to give courses in management, and to train a body of management teachers and management researchers, for all economic planning for national development would be a vain chimera unless productivity could be injected into our system. Planning, the British statesman Herbert Morrison once said, is but "applied commonsense". And productivity and management, too, cannot be quite outside the pale of commonsense. If achieved 'production' is indicative of economic growth, then 'productivity' is the dynamic condition that facilitates continuous and accelerating production of goods and services. Production is increased by material incentives, says one school of thought; it is increased rather by the impulsion of political and social idealism, says another school; but a third school – we may call it the technocratic – maintains that it is the injection of sound management techniques that really stimulates productivity.

Management acquires steadily increasing importance as we proceed from a traditional agricultural to a modern industrialised society. Agriculture was an integrated way of life and meant a creative participation of man with his environment. But modern industry is far more cunningly and complicatedly contrived. The power-driven machine is a new element in our lives, sometimes a helper, and sometimes an intruder if not an enemy. In cottage industries, as in agriculture, the producer (the artisan, the farmer) knows what he is doing, attends to the whole area of the productive process, and takes proper pride in his handiwork. On the other hand, under conditions of industrial mass production and exponential specialisation, the worker can have no total view or knowledge of the whole process and must needs be content with attending to his particular small segment of the involved sophisticated productive scenario. Not only has modern industry grown to be such a bewilderingly or frighteningly octopus-organisation, it has also to be sustained by equally complex collateral agencies of all kinds: say, for marketing the products, for siphoning finance, for maintaining public relations, for recruiting the labour force, for training the specialist technicians, and for conducting research facilitating the introduction of newer and still newer processes of production or more and more attractive baits for the avid consumerist society. And there are the Government Departments with their own confused and dilatory bureaucratic functioning, and there is increasing need to regulate the relationships between industry and the consumer (the people), and industry and the educational institutions. The net result is that a modern industrial society is essentially an aggregate of jobholders of all categories, some direct employees of the State, some of the public sector industries, some of the Defence establishments, and others of organisations and private industries that are controlled – or can be controlled – by the omnicompetent State in various open and not so easily perceived ways. Such a society of jobholders easily lends itself to regimentation, not caste-wise or profession-wise as of old, but as masters and men, as controllers and the controlled, as Boards of Directors and Labour Unions, as Faculties and student bodies. It is therefore argued that, even as there is more need for management in industry than in agriculture, and the bigger the industry the more is the need for management, in the modern State management has a role to play in all sectors of the economy and at all levels of administration.

It must be obvious, however, that management can have meaning only in relation to specified *ends*, and the *means* available (or mobilisable) to achieve these ends. We must have something to manage, and it is towards some end (the production of certain goods or the provision of specified services) that management is (or should be) directed. It is because the means – the human, physical and financial resources – are limited and the ends (or needs) are many (if not unlimited) that management is both necessary and difficult. Given the 'ends' or 'goals', management must consist in assembling the means, organising them to a condition of healthy productivity and maintaining such a condition, if not also steadily effecting further improvements.

These ideas are by no means so novel as they may be made to sound. Our hoary word 'Yoga' could mean 'addition', the injection or introduction of ideas or disciplines leading (as in catalysis) to a charging of power, a heightening of productivity and a quickening or enlargement of results. Yoga could lead to *kṣema*, the efflorescence of welfare. If work is worship, purposeful work could lead verily to Realisation. This truly is the heart of the matter. There can be no planning, no productivity, no management, no Loka Kshema or flowering of general prosperity, no Sarvodaya or sunrise of universal well-being, there can be none of these without a clear notion of the worthwhile goals and no less clear adhesion to the permissible means, without the readiness of people to work with a sense of common aims, a perceived sense of common direction and a converging feeling of total dedication.

II

Management is in the swim now in the higher academic world. There are the Institutes of Management and the University Faculties or Departments of Management offering sophisticated (and expensive) courses to aspirant managers and executives. Management specialisation is being pursued in respect of industry, agriculture, marketing, transportation, medicine, habitat, environment, education, Government and international relations. There are courses in Production Management, Management of Budget Planning and Control, Management of Public Health and Family Welfare, Management of Company Sales Force, Management of Conflict

Resolution in Industry, Management of Student (or faculty) Unrest, Management of Political Dissidence, Management of Karmachari Discontents, Management of Sudden Scarcity, and so on. But however valid and variegatedly differentiable all these exercises in nomenclature may be, it stands to reason that 'management' (call it art, science or mystique) is but one principle and power, although it may have endlessly varied applications in the promiscuously varying situations, circumstances and crises of life.

Basically, then, 'management' as an isolable force, technique or bag of tricks is supposed to have a catalytic effect on the efficient production of goods and services and on the regulation of relationships between different groups of people, especially groups within the same organisation, with a view to eliminating frictions and maximising goodwill and harmony. But if charity begins at home, so does management begin with oneself. Having won mastery of the three worlds, Hiranyakashipu the King of the Daityas felt that he was verily the omnipotent Lord. But his son, Prahlad, was bold enough to caution the King:

> Vain indeed is all overweening pride in the conquest even of the entire universe, if one has not conquered one's own passions!

Without the mastery of one's own ego, the containment of the turbulent enemy within, of what avail is the manipulation of mere techniques, or of the exercise of sovereignty over an outer empire? The Nigerian writer, Cyprian Ekwensi, shows in his novel 'Beautiful Feathers' that without self-mastery and "the backing of a family united by the bonds of love", one can hardly hope to render enduring public service. Self and Self-Management was the title of one of Arnold Bennett's popular guides, published about fifty years ago. The physician who can heal himself, the man who can master himself and manage efficiently his own affairs, starts under right auspices when he sets out on the career of management of others, and of institutions – small and large.

Administration or the art of management of men, affairs, institutions, situations and crises involves a background of knowledge, a sense of equity and the play of commonsense. The manager, the administrator, the leader should be able to make up his mind in a given situation, not whimsically, not yielding to sudden pressures or prejudices, but duly guided by a vision of the total unfolding possibility and armed with full knowledge and responsibility. In a cynical way, of course, one may deploy the four classic means of *sama-dama-daṇḍa-bheda*. There is the tactful and conciliating way littered with sweet speech: there is the way of bribing, carrot-waving, sugar plum offering: there is the devious divide and rule tactic: and there is the way of attack, revenge, deprivation, brandishing the big stick, giving no quarter. People are ordinarily moved by flattery, greed, suspicion and fear, and the manager, executive, administrator is free to exploit one or more or all of these only too common emotions and passions and inducements. But this may not take him far, or not for a long time, without hard-won knowledge, a gift of vision or feeling for perspective and a total sense of responsibility, one must sooner or later mess up 'management' and fail as administrator or shepherd of the flock.

It is clear that, for solving one's immediate problem, an unexpected development or a suddenly erupting crisis, one must not ignore the long-term consequences of what seems a tempting short-term remedy. Without commitment and a stern sense of responsibility, one may be apt to be swayed by the transient, and one's actions may become flawed, self-defeating and injurious to the institution in the long run.

In a predicament that calls for calm consideration of conflicting points of view and the fabrication of a viable as well as an acceptable solution, the short-term remedy being in no way repugnant to the long-term imperatives, the manager or executive or administrator cannot afford to behave like a helpless thistledown of random circumstances swaying this or that side according to the virulence of the raging winds. Generally in one's career as a manager, and more particularly in times of crises, one's motions and moves will necessarily be bound up with one's world-view or philosophy of life. There are, broadly speaking, two sharply distinct world-views that seem to hold the field. First, the materialist (or the individualist) view that thinks of the world as being made up of distinctive and independent building-blocks (electrons, protons, fermions, bosons, etc... and individuals, workers, citizens, students, etc.), and conveniently divides men into 'Us' and 'Them' in various degrees of opposition or confrontation. The commissar-managers ('Us') feel free to offer to the managed ('Them') financial and other incentives, hierarchical positions, status symbols (a car, a phone) and promotional possibilities; or to impose a stern discipline instilling fear as under a dictatorial dispensation (Emergency for ever!); or to modernise and rationalise the administration through the introduction of the latest machinery like dictaphones, intercom, computers, micro-processors, etc. for accomplishing the goal of fully integrated plant control or institutional ordering. More and more technological change, more and more sophistication, more and more substitution of human labour and expertise by electronic gadgetry, subtler and subtler ways of distancing the worker and the consumer from the entrepreneur and manager: these are the strategies with which 'We' try to hold our own against 'Them', the work force, the Union leaders, the rival entrepreneurs, the consumers, the Government officials. If a crisis erupts, 'We' try to deal with it in our way, and sometimes get away with it too.

A crisis usually builds up slowly, and often it is managerial complacency or labour intransigency that allows the crisis to get inflated to ominous proportions. Sometimes extraneous events – apparently altogether unrelated to the local situation – may spark off a crisis. A seizure of the American Embassy at Tehran or of the Grand Mosque at Mecca may have repercussions at Rawalpindi, New Delhi, Calcutta or Hyderabad. In the present-day world of instantaneous mass communication by radio or television, such instantaneous reactions (however irrational and destructive) cannot come as a surprise. Scientific and technological progress exposes us constantly to world happenings in all their incendiary detail, but our education hasn't given us the sobriety or maturity to react to such events with a due sense of decorum and responsibility. Even in a strictly local situation of labour or student or white-collar unrest, the manager or executive may be taken by surprise. The 'Us'/'Them' attitude of confrontation with the 'manager' and the 'others' on opposite sides of the barricades seldom leads to satisfactory solutions. Exploiting fear or greed, resorting to divide and rule (this against that group, one Union against another, one caste against another, one college or hostel against another) and bringing into play the seductions and blandishments of flattery are the common means adopted, but the success achieved is dubious and usually of very short duration. All over the world institutions continue to be bedevilled by discontent and unrest, and management is forced more often than not to be perpetually on the defensive, or to move from crisis to crisis, swinging between strikes and lockouts, police actions and arbitrations, and the manager can but continually keep his fingers crossed hoping for the best and yet afraid of the worst. One might almost throw up one's hands in despair and bemoan the current precarious state of affairs modifying the words of the poet:

> Where's the work we've scuttled through wild-cat
> strikes?
> Where are the strikes preempted by lockouts?
> The cycles of strike in all these hectic years
> Have brought us farther from peace and nearer to
> the dust.

III

When an individual (whether he be a labourer in a farm, a worker in a factory, a student in a college or university, a clerk in Government office, a technician in a national laboratory, or whether he is a landowner, manager of an industrial plant, a Principal or Vice-Chancellor, a secretary to a Government Department, or Director of a Laboratory), where an individual thinks of himself as an autonomous power that should thrive on his own wits, relying on himself alone or seeking an alliance with others similarly situated, but making a stand against the imagined antagonist or group of antagonists, this 'Us'/'Them' attritional confrontation, this paradigm of mutual exhaustion must prevail. Speaking some years ago on the Yogic approach to Administration to the Himachal Pradesh Secetariat Staff in Simla, Dr. Indra Sen remarked:

> There can be, one might say, two attitudes in general to life and life's work...
> There is the attitude of separate acquisition and possession, of competition, anxiety and strain....
> There is another one of relative freedom, of detachment, of relaxation and of self-consecration.

The latter attitude is born of a spiritual world-view, as distinct from the materialist (or building-blocks) world-view set forth in the earlier section. This spiritual world-view is illustrated by the bootstrap image of unity and intricate interdependence. If one accepts the building-blocks view of life, then one inevitably diminishes and enfeebles oneself into near-nothingness. In Kafka's symbolic story 'The Burrow', the protagonist desperately seeks security in an underground retreat with its manifold fortifications. But once one thus isolates oneself, how is ultimate safety to be secured? Was Parikshit really able to insulate himself from the 'Enemy'? If one must think of the Enemy, he is everywhere, and there can be no escape from him. Why not think of the Enemy as the Friend, why not transcend the duality of Enemy and Friend? As Kafka says in one of his aphorisms:

> He has two antagonists: the first pushing him from behind, from his birth. The second blocks the road in front of him. He struggles with both....

Two antagonists, and 'himself'; but can he not master and exceed both, as it were, become one with them? Isn't such identification and transcendence the true solution to his predicament?

Indeed, life is not a bundle of autonomous islands or entities, but an inextricably delicate web of infinite relationships. It is pervaded by the Divine; *īśāvāsyam idaṁ sarvam*. The Lord is in the heart of everything and all living beings:

> The Lord, O Arjuna, is seated in the heart of all beings, turning all beings mounted upon a machine by his Maya.[1]

Sri Aurobindo's comments on this verse are illuminating:

> ...when we enter into that inmost self of our existence, we come to know that in us and in all is the one Spirit and Godhead whom all Nature serves and manifests and we ourselves are soul of

this Soul, spirit of this Spirit, our body his dele-
gated image, our life a movement of the rhythm of
his life, our mind a sheath of his consciousness, our
senses his instruments, our emotions and sensa-
tions the seekings of his delight of being, our
actions a means of his purpose, our freedom only a
shadow, suggestion or glimpse while we are igno-
rant, but when we know him and ourselves a
prolongation and effective channel of his immortal
freedom. Our masteries are a reflection of his
power at work, our best knowledge a partial light
of his knowledge, the highest most potent will of
our spirit a projection and delegation of the will of
this Spirit in all things who is the Master and Soul
of the Universe.... And whether obscure in the
ignorance or luminous in the knowledge, it is for
him in us and him in the world that we have our
existence.[2]

The 'bootstrap' image of reality, as it has been put
forward by scientists like Geoffrey Chew, is apt because
it is well within our experience that the bootstrap cannot
be loosened anywhere without so loosening it everywhere, and it cannot be tightened up at any point
without a similar tightening up at every other point as
well: so complete and uncompromising is the unity and
interdependence. That the entire cosmos is an intricate
web of interpenetrating things and events is the insight
communicated in Avatamsaka Sutra by the myth of
Indra's net of pearls. "If you look at one", says Sir
Charles Eliot, "you see all others reflected in it. In the
same way each object in the world is not merely itself but

involves every other object and in fact is everything else."[3] Again as described in the same Sutra, Sudhana has a mystic experience of the universe as a complex of multitudinous towers in "a state of perfect intermingling and yet of perfect orderliness... all is contained in one and each contains all".[4] And this can be linked with Sri Aurobindo's conception of the 'supramental sense': "Nothing exists independently... but all is felt as one being and movement and each thing as indivisible from the rest and as having in it all the Infinite, all the Divine."[5] World-existence itself: what is it but "the ecstatic dance of Shiva which multiplies the body of the God numberlessly to the view"?[6] But the seeming multiplicity doesn't affect the unity of that 'white existence'!

If this be the deeper truth about omnipresent Reality, how about our little homestead, Earth? It is a little spaceship, and its inhabitants must float or crash together: there is no separate perdition or salvation for the blacks and the whites, for the commissars and the workers, for the teachers and the students. It is not as though the interests of one individual or group are really antagonistic to those of another or of another group. All can swim together, or all will sink together! The other man is not my enemy or opposite number; he is not even just my brother: he is, in fact, myself. This is the spiritual approach, and from this flows freedom, detachment, strength, relaxation and the urge for self-consecration.

The cardinal assumptions of the spiritual approach are interdependence, harmony, unity, creativity and evolutionary possibility. A bootstrap universe, yes; also, an evolutionary universe that wills and accomplishes self-change and continuous self-transformation. We are all in it: manager as well as the work-force, Vice-Chancellor as well as the faculty, students and ministerial staff, land-owners, as well as farmhands, commander-in-chief as well as the soldiers, the executive head as well as the rest of the establishment. Human beings at all points of the spectrum have to live and work with self-respect and enthusiasm. Thus while emoluments and material incentives and status inducements may have a place in this work-a-day world, even more to the purpose would be the commitment to service, creative collaboration with others and pride in the augmentation of work, wealth and happiness. Instead of trying to rule by suspicion, hatred and fear, the attempt to rule by the play of love, trust and mutual sympathy and understanding might prove more feasible and durable. Fear and hate poison the atmosphere and enfeeble and pervert the human instruments. In critical situations it would be more to the point to present a stance of strong immobility, a resolute screen that can fling back the vibrations of anger and misrepresentation and resentment and hatred. It is natural that people in perplexity should look for guidance to the Gita, which Sri Aurobindo has described as "the greatest gospel of spiritual works ever yet given to the race, the most perfect system of *Karmayoga* known to man in the past".[7] The 'equality' that the Gita enjoins is much more than mere "disappointed resignation", or defiant stoicism, or "a sage detachment"; the equality called for is verily "the

* As well as the faculty, students and ministerial staff, land-owner.

strong immobility of an immortal spirit".[8] As he explains it further:

> The equality spoken of is not indifference or impartiality or equability, but a fundamental oneness of attitude to all persons and all things and happenings because of the perception of all as the One... science and philosophy assure us of the same truth, that the universal is the Force which acts through the simulacrum of our individuality.[9]

In the course of one of her talks, the Mother too has commented on this sovereign mechanism of 'immobility':

> What the Gita wants is that the spirit should be conscious of its immortality and thus have a strong immobility... it is not an immobility of inertia or impotence; it is a strong immobility which is a basis for action.[10]

When a confrontation develops, the normal reaction is for anger to be met by anger, by fear, or ill-will, by more ill-will, or threatening aggressiveness by panic. Little is gained by such responses. The other way would be to meet hostile vibrations by a "complete immobility" that can be a protective wall of immense immaculate strength:

> ... If you can remain absolutely immobile within yourself... If you can remain like a wall, absolutely motionless, everything the other person sends you will immediately fall back upon him. And it has an immediate action. It can stop the arm of the

assassin... Only, one must not just appear to be immobile and yet be boiling inside.... I mean an integral immobility.[11]

But even such immobility by itself is not enough, though that is the indispensable starting-point. The confrontation has arisen on account of differences, prejudices, mutual misunderstandings, conflicting attitudes, crass or wrong-headed affirmations. Equality, immobility, inner renunciation of all adhesion to this or that result, these can prepare the ground: but an agreement has still to be hammered out and freely accepted by all. For this to have a chance of happening, the involved parties should try to rise to a higher than the average consciousness that is governed by irrationality, rise that is to the clear light of the higher reason where all irritations and clouded mental formations will disappear and the larger common interests will compel agreement and harmony. In the present-day world, what is happening only too often is that the disputants quickly gravitate to lower and lower depths of worse than bestiality, wielding the weapons of falsehood, prejudice, resentment, misrepresentation, anger; and before you know where you are, a point of no-return is reached, and one witnesses in a crescending sequence *dharnā*, *gherāo*, fighting, abuse, incendiarism and wanton destruction of all kinds. The Mother used to tell people who disagreed violently: "Come to agreement. That is the only way to do good work." But how is this to be done? Here is her ready answer:

For all to agree, each must rise to the top of his

> consciousness; it is on the heights that harmony is created.
>
> When we have to work collectively, it is always better to insist, in our thoughts, feelings and actions, on the points of agreement rather than on the points of difference.
>
> We must give importance to the things that unite, and ignore as much as possible those that separate.[12]

Not disagreement and division, not even merely a patched-up compromise, but reconciliation, wholeness and harmony: that is the way to cultivate, "the only way to do good work". Various forms of communal life that bring 'Us' and 'Them' together – sports, music and entertainment, congregational worship and prayer, co-operative work as service or as offering untainted by personal reward or egoistic pride – can cleanse the flawed human sensibility of its falsity and hypocrisy and vain self-deceiving.

It may be asked: Isn't all this, however unexceptionable in theory, too difficult to put into practice and realise fully in everyday life? No doubt, whatever is ideally desirable is also extremely difficult, but one must make a beginning with faith and hope, and take the decisive turn in one's life. At least the commissaristic attitude of 'Us'/'Them' (and 'I'/'You') could progressively be leavened by the spiritual or Yogic approach. After all, over a period of several million years, humanity has moved from backwardness to civilisation, and man has been adventuring in the arts of peace and the arts of war. And this march towards new horizons is not ended.

The last few decades have witnessed the revolutionary breakthroughs in physical science and molecular biology. The atom has been smashed and nuclear energy has been released alike for destructive and peaceful purposes. The genetic code has been unravelled and we are on the threshold of momentous new discoveries in the field of 'life'. After 'matter' and 'life' – 'mind' – and we are perhaps on the eve of a like breakthrough in the realm of 'mind', a possible explosion of human consciousness that will enlarge its vision and heighten its power. In the result, matching the revolutionary metamorphoses in 'matter' and 'life' the human personality itself may undergo a radical transformation, and the 'Us'/'Them' segregation, instead of being divided by egoistic separativity, falsity and antagonism, may be able to achieve instinctive empathy and understanding, teaming together and marching towards the beckoning goals of fulfilment. And that will make possible an ideal system of human relationships or the future 'ideal management'.

IV

Sri Aurobindo's stress on the importance of the Gita as a manual of *Karma Yoga* has been referred to already. The celebrated affirmation *yogaḥ karmasu kauśalam* is a deceptively reassuring theorem of Yogic action and realisation. And what does it mean precisely? What is 'kaushalam' or 'skill'? No more than a sleight of hand? A sort of uncanniness or instinctive accuracy? It is of course a very different order of 'skill' that Krishna has in mind, as may be seen from these words of Sri Aurobindo:

> ... the liberated who has united his reason and will with the Divine... rises to a higher law beyond good and evil, founded in the liberty of self-knowledge... action done in Yoga is not only the highest but the wisest, the most potent and efficient even for the affairs of the world; for it is informed by the knowledge and will of the Master of works: 'Yoga is skill in works'.[13]

Others are side-tracked and distracted by the sense of ego, of mine and thine, but the Yogin is emancipated from such prison-houses, and feels electrically and seraphically free:

> He acts as others, but he has abandoned all desires and their longings. He attains to the great peace and is not bewildered by the shows of things; he has extinguished his individual ego in the One, lives in that unity and, fixed in that status at his end, can attain to extinction in the Brahman, Nirvana, – not the negative self-annihilation of the Buddhists, but the great immergence of the separate personal self into that vast reality of the one infinite impersonal Existence.[14]

There is no running away from action, nor any weakening of the power or effectivity of the action; by conscious contact or union with the Divine, it is as though a diminutive brook has been connected with a mighty Himalayan reservoir, immaculate and inexhaustible. In one of his aphorisms, Sri Aurobindo insinuates his meaning with a singular quirk of sensibility:

The path of works is in a way the most difficult side of God's triune causeway; yet is it not also, in this material world at least, the easiest, widest and most delightful? For at every moment we clash against God the worker and grow into His being by a thousand divine touches.[15]

In the Gita,[16] Krishna says that although, being the Divine, he is beyond the need to do or gain anything in all the three worlds, still he ceaselessly engages in action as part of the cosmic play with the result that we too, as we labour in our own imperfect way, come into contact with him and his work; and this participation, however unconscious at first, can grow more and more into conscious collaboration, till at last the two become indistinguishable. The Lord seems to say:

'I abide in the path of action,' ... ' the path that all men follow.... In the way I act, in that way thou too must act.... The whole range of human action has been decreed by Me with a view to the progress of man from the lower to the higher nature, from the apparent undivine to the conscious Divine.... All individual, all social action, all the works of the intellect, the heart and the body are still his, not any longer for his own separate sake, but for the sake of God in the world, of God in all beings...'[17]

The core of the problem, whether of self-management or of management of others, is self-change and world-change through the process and power of Yoga. In his essay "Yoga and Skill in Works," Sri Aurobindo writes:

> Yoga is the exchange of an egoistic for a universal
> or cosmic consciousness lifted towards or informed
> by the supracosmic, transcendent Unnameable
> who is the source and support of all things. Yoga is
> the passage of the human thinking animal towards
> the God-consciousness from which he has des-
> cended."[18]

Where the self-cabined egoistic 'I'/'We' attitude per-
sists, where the 'Us'/'Them' antagonism dims every-
body's vision, where desire, agitation, passion, pain and
tension strain at the ego, confusions and distortions are
inevitably introduced, and all action is flawed or is at
cross-purposes; all such action is unskilled, imperfect
and ineffective. But the consciousness of a Yogin that is
enfranchised from the ego-shell or Kafkaesque 'burrow'
has a new puissance and universality and infallibility.
Such a Yogin rears on the foundation of his perfect
equality the force of universality that beyonds his own
limited body, temperament and mind, and feels one
with the Divine:

> It is evident that such an increasing wideness of
> vision must mean an increasing knowledge. And if
> it be true that knowledge is power, it must mean
> also an increasing force for works.[19]

With the silencing of the normal functioning of the
mind, the play of desire, will and passions at the behest
of the ego is hushed up, and other faculties, illumina-
tions, powers come into the scene operating from the
higher-than-the-mind levels of consciousness, and thereby

"increase the force, subtlety and perfection of the Yogin's skill in works".[20] In course of time and in the high plenitude of the Yogin's life, there is bound to be a splendorous change in the whole quality and intensity of his 'skill in works', and in his flair for perfect management in all the conceivable situations of life. At last 'skill' in works will also be sheer delight in works, and the Yogin's works will be charged with beauty, power and glory revealing the triune handiwork of Varuna, Mitra and Aryaman – "Aryaman's power, Mitra's love and light, Varuna's unity".[21]

The Lord of the Gita says that he continually abides in the path of action keeping the worlds going. When Wordsworth apostrophises Duty:

> Thou dost preserve the stars from wrong;
> And the most ancient heavens, through Thee, are
> fresh and strong!...

he is really addressing Shakti, the ordaining power behind Nature. While describing the powers and personalities of the Mother, Sri Aurobindo visualises Maheshwari laying down "the large lines of the world-forces", Mahakali charging them with "energy and impetus", and Mahalakshmi discovering "their rhythms and measures". The bold imaginative planning, the installation of the Power House of the spirit for channelising the needed energy, and the forging on the heaving mass the forms and curves of beauty and significance are important enough. But equally important is the need for patience and perseverance in organisation and execution, the infallible sense of detail, the deploying of the right elements and instruments and agents in right measure and at the right time to yield the desired results; all this is Mahasaraswati's prerogative:

> Always she holds in her nature and can give to those whom she has chosen the intimate and precise knowledge, the subtlety and patience, the accuracy of intuitive mind and conscious hand and discerning eye of the perfect worker. This Power is the strong, the tireless, the careful and efficient builder, organiser, administrator, technician, artisan and classifier of the worlds. When she takes up the transformation and new-building of the nature, her action is laborious and minute and often seems to our impatience slow and interminable, but it is persistent, integral and flawless. For the will in her works is scrupulous, unsleeping, indefatigable; leaning over us she notes and touches every little detail, finds out every minute defect, gap, twist, or incompleteness, considers and weighs accurately all that has been done and all that remains still to be done hereafter.... In her constant and diligent arrangement and rearrangement of things her eye is on all needs at once and the way to meet them and her intuition knows what is to be chosen and what rejected and successfully determines the right instrument, the right time, the right conditions and the right process.... When her work is finished, nothing has been forgotten, no part has been misplaced or omitted or left in a faulty condition... Nothing short of a perfect perfection satisfies her and she is ready to face an eternity of toil if that is

needed for the fullness of her creation.[22]

The Mother, too, is the Divine, but in the more easily visible, more reassuringly approachable aspect of Shakti or Consciousness-Force; she is in a sense the Power visualised by Wordsworth as Duty, and she is rather significantly the ambrosial front that presents in its immediacy and total efficacy the supreme Grace of the Divine. The Yogic infallible strategy, then would be to make the definitive choice, to mount "a fixed and unfailing aspiration" from below, to purify one's instruments, to minimise and then throw out the false and likewise to maximise the good, and to offer all oneself and one's efforts and the fruits (and failures) of one's actions to the Divine, all the while waiting on Grace, for the answering gift of Grace from the Supreme. During the process of Yoga, there is a progressive detachment from the pulls of one's egoistic exclusiveness and a progressive identification with the Divine, or (as in the Tantric tradition) with the Divine Mother. This will engineer the desired alchemy, and the Yogin will realise more and more that, not he, but the Mother – or one of her Powers and Personalities – is the effective actor and executant, the human worker being only the willing agent or instrument:

> The last stage of this perfection will come when you are completely identified with the Divine Mother and feel yourself to be no longer another and separate being, instrument, servant or worker but truly a child and eternal portion of her consciousness and force. Always she will be in you and

you in her; it will be your constant, simple and natural experience that all your thought and seeing and action, your very breathing or moving come from her and are hers.... When this condition is entire and her supramental energies can freely move you, then you will be perfect in divine works; knowledge, will, action will become sure, simple, luminous, spontaneous, flawless, an outflow from the Supreme, a divine movement of the Eternal.[23]

When the sadhak, the Yogin, attains – or even approaches – this summit of constant identification and unification with the Mother, he will be able to act with instinctive knowledge, power, ease and precision. It is immaterial whether he wields the Field Marshal's baton or carries the farmer's plough, whether he is charged with the management of a large factory or he is absorbed in following the sinuous movements of a sub-atomic particle, whether he has to tackle and quieten an agitated and unruly mob of workers or he has to find the right words to transcribe the contours of a fugitive dream. What ever the challenge or opportunity, he has won the crown of equality, he has scuttled the obstreperous ego-sense, and he has invoked the Divine to fill the vacuum created by the death of the ego. And, in course of time, the prophecy made in *Savitri* may be realised after all:

More and more souls shall enter into light,
Minds lit, inspired, the occult summoner hear
And lives blaze with a sudden inner flame
And hearts grow enamoured of divine delight

And human wills tune to the divine will,
These separate selves the Spirit's oneness feel,
These senses of heavenly sense grow capable,
The flesh and nerves of a strange ethereal joy
And mortal bodies of immortality.[24]

DR. K. R. SRINIVASA IYENGAR

References:

1. *Gita*, Ch. XVIII, Verse 61. Translation from the *Message of the Gita* (1977), edited by A.B. Roy.
2. *Essays on the Gita* (Cent. Ed., Vol. 13), p. 535.
3. Quoted in Fritjof Capra, *The Tao of Physics*, Fontana, 1976, p. 314.
4. *Ibid.*, p. 310.
5. *The Synthesis of Yoga* (Cent. Ed., Vol. 20), pp. 834-35.
6. *The Life Divine* (Cent. Ed., Vol. 18), p. 78.
7. *The Synthesis of Yoga* (Cent. Ed., Vol. 20), p. 87.
8. *Ibid.*, p. 95.
9. *The Supramental Manifestation* (Cent. Ed., Vol. 16), p. 294.
10. *Questions and Answers*, 1956 (Cent. Ed., Vol. 8), p. 66.
11. *Ibid.*, pp. 67-68.
12. *Words of The Mother* (Cent. Ed., Vol. 14), p. 335.
13. *Essays on the Gita* (Cent. Ed., Vol. 13), p. 96.
14. *Ibid.*, p. 97.
15. *The Hour of God* (Cent. Ed., Vol. 17), p. 124.
16. Ch. III, Verse 22.
17. *Essays on the Gita* (Cent. Ed., Vol. 13), pp. 130-1.
18. *The Supramental Manifestation* (Cent. Ed., Vol. 16), p. 291.
19. *Ibid.*, p. 295.
20. *Ibid.*, p. 296.
21. *Ibid.*, p. 297.
22. *The Mother* (Cent. Ed., Vol. 25), pp. 33-34.
23. *Ibid.*, pp. 17-18.
24. *Savitri* (Cent. Ed., Vol. 29), p. 710.

3

MANAGEMENT BY INTUITION

Tomorrow's managers will face extremely complex situations in which they will need to make decisions under circumstances where the complete data necessary for traditional decision-making processes will be unavailable, inadequate, or too costly to gather quickly.

They will be dealing with a changing world and a work-force that will make increasing demands for real participation in the decision-making process. Managers will need to rely less on formal authority and more on intuitive judgement in order to handle the shift to bottom-up, horizontal organisational communication with sensibility and persuasiveness.

Managers will need a new set of skills to cope with this shifting environment. Until now, the predominant management approach has been the logical, analytical, 'left-brain' style. Business and public administration schools across the United States have stressed linear, deductive reasoning based on case studies of problem-solving.

But a new model is developing, one patterned after the emerging successful Japanese management style that blends analysis with insight. Shigeru Okada, head of one of Japan's largest departmental stores, explained the reason for his company's success in *The American Banker*: "It was due to our adoption of the West's pragmatic management combined with spiritual, intuitive aspects of the East".

More and more leaders are coping with rapid changes

by sharpening their intuitive, inductive skills, and intuition's value in business and management is already becoming clear. Over a period of two years, I tested the intuitive abilities of more than 2,000 managers across the United States at all levels of responsibility, in a wide variety of organisations – business, government, education, military and health. The findings are dramatic. According to Sri Aurobindo there are ascents to Supermind – the levels, according to him, being Higher Mind – Illumined Mind – Intuitive Mind – Over Mind – Supermind. Intuition, according to Sri Aurobindo, "is always an edge or ray or outleap of a superior light; it is in us a projecting blade, edge or point of a far-off supermind... substance above us...

Intuition has a fourfold power. A power of revelatory truth-seeing, a power of inspiration or truth-hearing, a power of truth-touch... a power of true and automatic discrimination of the orderly and exact relation of truth to truth... Intuition can therefore perform all the action of reason, – including the function of logical intelligence, which is to work out the right relation of things and the right relation of idea with idea, – but by its own superior process and with steps that do not fail or falter."*

Without exception, the top managers in every organisation rated significantly higher than middle and lower managers in their ability to use intuition on the job to make decisions.

Executives use intuition in a variety of ways. According to *American Banker*, Robert Bernstein, chairman of Random House, believes that "only intuition can protect

* *The Life Divine* (Cent. Ed., Vol. 19), pp. 948-949.

you from the most dangerous individual – the articulate individual incompetent".

William G. Mcginnis, the city manager of Crescent City, California, relies on his intuition in public meetings when he has to make immediate judgements. For example, in a city council meeting, he will often size up the reaction of the council members as they listen to testimony on alternative proposals and base his recommendations on his intuitive assessment of what the council will find acceptable. "When you have to react quickly with intuitive thought processes you base your decision on what's occurred in the past," he says.

Successful executives tend to rely less on fact-gathering and more on their instincts. Any time decisions must be made quickly or an issue is so complex that complete information is not available, the managers who have developed their intuition will have an advantage over those who have not. And in the rapidly changing, complex world of the future, these situations will be more and more common.

Just what is this mysterious process? Psychologist Carl Jung calls intuition one of the four basic psychological functions, along with thinking, feeling and sensation. It is the function that "explores the unknown and senses possibilities and implications which may not be readily apparent."

Webster's dictionary defines it as "the act or process of coming to direct knowledge or certainty without reasoning or inferring; immediate apprehension or cognition."

But it may be better understood with a more personal definition. For example, frequently we have an intuitive understanding of a person or a situation but are afraid to act on the basis of this instant awareness. Instead, we play the mental "tape" we have been socialised to follow: "you had better wait, gather more facts, get to know the situation better." Thus we delay decisions and actions, pushing our immediate impressions of situations into our subconscious. Only after actual day-to-day experience with a person or situation do we allow our feelings to surface to our conscious mind and we come to realise that those initial instincts that we failed to act upon were correct.

"That little voice inside you is the distillate of all your experiences", says Richards Brown, former president of Towle Manufacturing, who bases many of his decisions on intuition.

Fully developed intuition is highly efficient – a way of knowing immediately. It is fast and accurate. We can process a wide array of information on many levels and gain instantaneous clues as to how to act. We have the answer although we do not understand all the types or know how our mental system processed the information.

Intuitive abilities will become more and more valuable during the coming period of surprises, complexities and rapid changes. The organisations of tomorrow will require a breed of executives trained in these decision-making techniques.

Signs are already evident that management education programmes are beginning to create courses designed to develop intuitive skills. For example, the Stanford University Business School is currently offering a course on "Creativity in Business" that emphasises the right-brain approach. By 1995, the leading management training programmes, both private and public, are likely to place just as much emphasis on the training of intuitive, precognitive right-brain skills as they presently do on deductive, analytical left-brain skills.

As businesses realise the potential of intuition and the importance of these other brain skills, they will learn how to use personality tests and other methods to match an individual's brain skills with job requirements in ways that can raise both productivity and job satisfaction. The kind of brain skills needed for various jobs vary by organisational type, level of management and occupational specialisation, with some tasks calling for left-brain skills and still others for integrative skills that combine both kinds of thinking.

An individual's particular abilities can be determined using a combination of tests. A basic personality test can help determine what kinds of occupations would be most appropriate for an individual. The organisation might then administer a portion of the Myers-Briggs Personality Inventory that measures the person's potential capacity to use intuition in decision-making. Finally, the brain skills – left, integrative, or right – a person is actually using on the job to make decisions can be tested.

This testing of new employees could aid greatly in the process of selecting and placing personnel.

From the employees' point of view, Daniel Girdano and George Everly report in Controlling Stress and Tension that workers' health is closely linked to whether their brain skills are properly matched to their jobs; whether they are in touch with their dominant brain styles; and whether they are in fact using their dominant brain styles on the job. An organisation with an effective placement programme that takes into account brain styles and position requirements will benefit from the decrease in health costs normally borne by individuals and their organisations.

Knowledge of brain skills can improve a company's productivity in other ways, as well. Test results can be used to choose work-teams for various projects in ways that enhance maximum performance. Such factors as the degree of intuitive or analytical skills required, the most advantageous mix of brain types and the personality types that would ensure the most effective team effort can be taken into account.

Brain-style testing can also improve communication within an organisation. For example, at Walt Disney Enterprises the creative people had a hard time understanding and communicating with the production and financial group – and vice versa. The intuitive "imagineers" – the artists, writers and craftsmen – approached the problem quite differently from the analytical "engineers" or "financiers". The rift began to heal and communication began to improve only after each group saw the results of the brain-style tests and understood the basis for their colleagues' thoughts and actions.

Individuals will also find ways that their own careers can benefit from brain-style testing. My own test results indicate that those managers with higher levels of intuitive ability are likely to be particularly effective in such fields as personnel, health, public affairs, advertising, public relations, marketing, and crisis management – areas that demand imagination, creativity and other right-brain skills.

Women and those with Asian background score consistently higher in intuitive ability, suggesting that members of these groups should consider actively developing and marketing their intuitive skills as an effective vehicle for career advancement in the organizations of tomorrow.

All too frequently, we reject new and different ways of solving problems because we are accustomed to a particular way of doing things. Often it is only in crises – business failures, loss of health or loved ones – that we reach for alternative methods, allowing our inherent intuitive skills to surface and be of assistance to us. Fortunately, however, we do not need to experience serious traumas in order to develop our intuitive ability. Individuals interested in using intuition on the job or for career advancement will find that there are several techniques for development of their ability.

Intuition becomes more efficient as we become more open to our feelings and more secure through experience in its ability to provide the correct cues. The first rule is to believe in it. What we believe we can do is one of the most important factors in determining what we can in fact do. For example, chief executive officers who believe in their ability to make decisions guided by intuition also have the highest profit record, according to a report by Douglas Dean and John Mihalasky in Executive ESP.

The second rule is practice makes perfect. We all possess the ability to use intuition to make decisions, but all too frequently we fail to develop our capacity to the fullest. A blind person can develop his or her sense of touch to the extent of "seeing" colours through sensing the relative degree of heat given off by the intensity of hues. With effort and persistence, we can develop our intuition in the same way.

The third rule is to create a supportive environment in which intuitive skills are valued. There are test exercises and games – involving such techniques as meditation, guided imagery and dream analysis – that serve to focus our attention within rather than without.

More executives and organisations are likely to embrace such positive efforts to increase intuitive abilities as the need for new skills to cope with the shifting organisational climate increases. Managers who continue to rely solely on empirical evidence that has been sifted, digested and analysed may lose out to the leaders who have the confidence and competence to follow their intuitive instincts in times of rapid change.

WESTON H. AGOR

4

CONSCIOUSNESS APPROACH TO BUSINESS MANAGEMENT – I

Men, Materials & Methods

The Consciousness Approach is applicable to any field of human activity. Before considering in depth the specific case of Business Management, let us discuss the fundamental principle upon which the entire approach is based and consider its wider application in the life of an individual. We do so because there can be no clear division between a man's personal and professional life; the two overlap and constantly interact.

This principle denotes that there is a direct correspondence between man's inner life of thoughts, feelings and impulses – his consciousness – and the circumstances and events in his outer environment. The external situation is an extension of his inner consciousness expressed in outer life. This principle is derived from the most universally accepted spiritual knowledge, the truth of Oneness. There is but One Reality which manifests itself as many. All are essentially One. The sense of separation, independence, difference is a surface phenomenon. Yet even on the surface all beings, things and events are linked in mutual inter-dependence. Man's ego acts as a knot dividing the individual from the world around, the inner from the outer. But the fact of oneness remains. This principle implies a very powerful tool for affecting the external world by discovering the point in one's consciousness which corresponds to an outer condition and acting on that point by an inner effort. Normally life events are a reaction to one's inner condition. When a conscious effort is made to change oneself within, life responds to that effort.

If one scrupulously examines the events of a single day in the light of his thoughts, feelings, impulses, a pattern of correspondence will begin to reveal itself. This knowledge can gradually be extended to include all the conditions, circumstances, events in his personal and professional life. Then by a firm decision in the mind or an intense will in the heart one can modify his thoughts, feelings, impulses. He can replace negative attitudes, biased opinions, impatient expectations, confused rambling thoughts with clear, objective, positive mentation or even silent receptivity which allows a higher understanding to be born. He can reject turbulent feelings, insatiable desires, possessiveness and selfish demand to attain a calm, peaceful, harmonious condition in which the deeper emotions of sympathy, goodwill, self-giving and love can emerge. To the degree that this inner mastery and perfection is achieved, outer conditions and events take on a strongly positive and co-operative character. Life brings constant opportunity and fulfils every requirement. The area of one's effectivity depends upon the development of his consciousness and the field of outer life with which he concerns himself, identifies in thought and emotion. It is most powerful in the close proximity of one's personal environment, family, home and profession. As the consciousness grows, expands, enlarges to identify itself with wider fields of human activity, there is an increasing capacity to affect the greater life of the society. This type of effort falls within the domain of Yoga.

In business these correspondences can be seen in all aspects of institutional operation, most easily perhaps in the relationship between management's attitudes and feelings on specific issues and the behaviour of employees. For example, it is a common complaint of management that staff are not interested in the quality of work they do, only in the monetary rewards for the job. Yet in almost all such cases it can be easily verified that the manager is not at all interested in the individual worker for his own sake, only in his productivity. Both look after their own interest and do not bother about any greater good. In unusual cases where the manager truly takes interest in each individual, in his health, welfare, creativity and happiness, the workers are very much concerned about the quality of the work performed and the success of the entire enterprise. In either case the attitudes and behaviour of the employees toward work are a direct reflection of management's attitudes toward them.

Another common situation is one in which management concerns itself with the happiness and welfare of its employees only when a crisis comes, such as a threatening walk-out or a strike. The corresponding employee attitude is a refusal to work without constant supervision and reprimand. In either case a sincere attempt by the organizational heads to reverse their attitudes will bring about an immediate change in the behaviour of the staff.

There are any number of examples for this principle, for it expresses itself in an infinite number of ways through every aspect of life. All of the other principles derive from this truth. These separate principles are considered because it is easier for the mind to see life from a single viewpoint and each of these principles looks at the Oneness of Life from a different angle. If one becomes directly aware of the One divine Reality through the practice of Yoga, then all mental principles fall away before the clear perception of the true relationship between all the manifold elements of existence.

All of the illustrations which follow are from the author's personal experience testing these principles in actual practice both in India and in the United States.

II

An institution cannot be properly described by categorizing it solely in terms of a business, social, political or educational function. It is much closer to the truth that an institution is a living organism with a personality, history, life experiences, skills and capabilities all its own. The original founding idea, concept or ideal, the pioneering individual, the social and economic climate and context, the prior condition of the field in which it is established, all contribute to determining the character of the institution even in the distant future. All present attributes can be traced back to their seed origin in the past. In Sri Aurobindo's terms, each institution has a mental part composed of the constituting ideals, principles and rules for governing its operations, decision-making processes and systems of communication. It has a vital part composed of the energies and dynamic processes which translate plan into action and yield concrete results and it has a physical part, the building,

equipment, tools and machines. The individuals employed by an institution contribute their own personal
qualities and resources to these different levels. But
besides these, every institution is like every individual
and every nation, an evolving being which has behind
and within it a higher element of divinity, a soul-spark.
Like the individual and the nation, the institution can
only fulfill itself by discovering this element, bringing all
its life into conformity with that living ideal and expressing it in daily functioning. In short, every institution
regardless of its nature – political, social, religious and
economic – has a role to play in the growth of those who
participate in it, a role to play in the growth of the larger
community of which it is a part, a rightful seeking for its
own fullest and highest development as a manifestation
of some aspect of divinity. A business institution is a
living organism and, like any person, it responds to us.

The practical value of this viewpoint is immense when
rightly applied to a specific institution, a business for
instance. First, it makes for a much truer awareness of
exactly what the business is and the important role
played by so many factors in forming its present make-
up. With individuals, it is natural to attribute a particular
personality characteristic to a childhood circumstance or
other life events. Such an approach yields a fuller
comprehension of who the individual is. The same is
true of an institution. Secondly, this approach provides a
key for the proper understanding and resolution of
specific problems in the present. A company is depen-
dent on but not limited by any element such as owner,
manager, expertise, sales potential, etc., though all of
these contribute to its character and may powerfully

influence its very existence. Whoever seeks to truly know the company or fully relate to it, whether he is management, staff, client, etc., can best do so by recognizing this truth and seeking contact with the central personality. Furthermore, to the extent that anyone does relate to the central personality and identify with it, to that extent he gains influence over all aspects of its present existence and future destiny. One individual taking sincere interest can change the functioning of a large enterprise. All depends on the degree of his interest and the application of his will.

III

There is no matter animate or inanimate that does not respond to attention. In an institution the employees, the ideals, systems of functioning, rules, machinery, material and physical space all require a certain minimum of attention and all of them will respond to increased attention by serving better. The result is most pronounced where the attention given is motivated simply by respect and concern for the thing and without demand or expectation. The truth is that the Divine is in all things and all things are Divine. By giving attention in the form of mental interest, loving concern, enthusiasm, physical care, we contact and respect the Divine in matter. Let us consider the role of attention in a number of areas.

Attention to Employees

We have stated earlier that attention given to men

creates interest in work. To elaborate, one can see an individual as a whole person and not just in his role as employee, try to know and understand his life circumstances, his goals, strengths, habits, weaknesses, likes and dislikes, problems, attitude towards work, his feelings towards the work. One can treat him according to this knowledge with due respect for his ideas and feelings, desires and needs, interest in his development, concern for his growth, happiness, health and well-being. One can translate this knowledge and feeling into concrete attempts to help him whenever that falls within the reasonable scope of one's means and does not threaten to cause undue problems in the relationship between management and staff. It is true that certain rules, positions and formalities should be respected and maintained in behaviour but that does not limit one's capacity to understand and sympathize and should not be used as an excuse for hardness and indifference towards those who serve one. The best means to give attention to men is to take interest in the work that they do and give just recognition, and in that context to provide each worker with the opportunity to constantly learn new skills and obtain new knowledge and exercise new responsibilities appropriate to his capacities. It is possible to provide even the lowliest of workers with the opportunity for advancement by setting clearly before him the steps to perfection in his present work and presenting new opportunities when that perfection is reached. No worker can remain indifferent to the sincere concern of the employer for his growth and well-being. He will definitely respond by showing that same concern in his execution of the work. What responsibility one inwardly feels and accepts for his life, he will automatically feel and express in his work. The inner concern must be genuine but in outer expression the attention should be limited by the extent to which he identifies himself with the work. One will find that when his inner attitude is proper, this identification will follow of itself. Give him the attention he deserves.

One's success can be measured by the effect on an employee's non-work life — either creatively by preparing him for a better job or encouraging him to further education, or at least functionally in terms of his manners, conscience, behaviour, family life, etc. One should encourage the progress of emloyees even if it seems to be away from the company. Encourage all expansive movements.

There are a number of criteria to ensure that each man receives the attention he deserves:

1. He should be considered as a human being more than as an employee;

2. The job he does should result in psychological satisfaction making him desire to have more work;

3. He should find constantly newer skills added to his capacity;

4. His work-pattern should include a built-in recreation that prevents accumulation of frustration or tension;

5. His work should help to harness all his energies and give them to the work so that tedium, except the physical part, will be minimal;

6. There should be a genuine appreciation and psychological recognition of talents when they are found or freshly emerge. Work must help to reveal and develop these talents.

There is a negative side to attention as well:

1. No man should be given even a little more than he deserves; he must not be in a position to take from the management more than is his due;

2. No more interest should be given than the person's psychological identification warrants;

3. No man should be employed in such a way that only a part of his capacities are utilised. This gives him extra energies which often express themselves in a manner detrimental to the work;

4. No man should be at any work requiring him to give an excessive effort which may create tension and spread to other men;

5. The surest way of bringing trouble into any relationship is to give someone more than what he deserves.

There are cases in which attention should not be given. A manager of a large government service bureau in California complained about the behaviour of one of his staff who kept his office in a state of complete chaos, who was always speaking in a loud and crude language to the staff members, interrupting and contradicting them in staff conferences and disagreeing with the manager on every possible occasion. From a description of his behaviour it was obvious that all this was done merely to gain attention from the manager and other employees. In such cases attention should definitely not be given to these negative expressions which only reinforce occurrence. Rather they should be completely ignored. Efforts should be made to identify the underlying sources of the problem and attention applied either silently within oneself or in conjunction with external measures to remove the trouble.

There are innumerable examples illustrating the benefit which results from acting out of compassion, understanding, patience, goodwill, leniency with the faults of others, giving people the freedom to make mistakes and the chance to exercise responsibility. All such qualities will prove a great asset in any work, only they must be applied with one qualification. To the extent that a man identifies himself with the work project, feels a part of it, sincerely works for its progress, both the work and his own personality will benefit from this attitude. Where a man is only interested in himself or is hostile, one may still be compassionate but not allow him to unduly jeopardise the work. It is wrong to exploit others. It is equally wrong to let others exploit you.

Successful industrialists often respond to this point by saying that they have seen it proved in their own business in the early stages when the staff was small and close personal contact with each worker was possible. The men worked enthusiastically and took pride in the production. But later when business expanded and the labour force doubled or tripled in size, it was no longer possible to get to know every man and attend to him. Then the outside unions come in and everything is further depersonalized. The answer to this is for management to continue to give the same close attention to those with whom they work, to their supervisory staff, aides, etc. and in turn to instil the same attitude in these people, encouraging them to take active interest in the lives of those whom they have responsibility for in the work. A manager of 20 men can know each one very well. When the staff expands to 200 he can still take lively interest in twenty and each of them can relate to 20 men under them. It is possible to develop a hierarchy of personal relationship and genuine attention.

Outward attention to another is of limited value if it becomes a matter of policy or habit rather than an expression of genuine inner concern. Yet even in this form it is far better than unconsciousness towards others. Best of all is to strive towards an awareness of the true inner person behind another's appearance, gestures, words, thoughts and feelings. This can only come about by a corresponding effort at self-knowledge and self-discovery. Behind the personality of every man the soul resides, a spark of the Divine. By contacting that point in oneself and relating to that same point in others, one will spontaneously bring forth the best qualities in others. They will offer maximum co-operation and reap maximum growth.

Attention to Other Living Beings

Recently there has been an increasing amount of literature about the sensitivity of plants to various types of human stimulation, thought, emotion and touch as well as their response to mechanical stimuli. It is a fact that plants are conscious, though not with the normal human mentality or emotions, and they are highly receptive to mental, emotional and nervous vibrations as well as various forms of physical energy. Like people, plants respond to all positive vibrations – thoughts for their welfare, happy emotions, peace, calm and harmony, etc. They express this response by their rate of growth and the quality and quantity of flowers and fruits. It has also been documented that certain negative vibrations like fear, anger, loud noise or violent chaotic music cause retardation of their development. What is true for plants is even more true for animals.

Attention to Tools and Machines

When a tool breaks or a machine is constantly in need of repair or some item is lost — all these are warnings that one's attention to these things has not been adequate. Constant use is attention to material things. As with living things so with inanimate objects. Not only our outer handling of them but also the thoughts and feelings or unconsciousness we have concerning them affect their performance and life-span. It is true from our side that an active concern leads to better handling and maintenance. It is also true that concern elicits an active response from the objects themselves. They serve better and even if lost find their way back. For all matter, not only plants, animals and men, possess a consciousness. But while in living organisms the consciousness manifests itself as growth, movement, sensitivity, feeling, thought, etc., in inanimate matter it is involved and invisible to sense perception. Nevertheless all matter responds to the consciousness of beings near to it. Also like the living organisms, it is in its essence Divine. If one has progressed far enough in his own conscious development, the inner consciousness of inanimate objects and their response to conscious attention is a matter of everyday experience. Many famous spiritual personalities have been known to treat the objects around them as if they were living beings and there are numerous stories of how the objects have responded by performing far longer than is normally possible without wearing out.

Not only objects but areas of space, rooms and buildings respond to attention. Naturally in most cases the response is more subtle, less easily perceptible. Yet most people are aware that some places have a nicer "atmosphere" than others. In some, one feels more comfortable, better able to concentrate, more relaxed, happier, more alert. These qualities are directly attributable to the consciousness of the individuals who normally occupy the place and to the manner of their behaviour. Cleanliness, orderliness, absence of loud sounds or of the expression of anger, positive thoughts and feelings, the presence of beautiful music or fresh flowers, all contribute to creating a positive atmosphere. Once created, this atmosphere actually responds by discouraging the occurrence of such events or the approach of such behaviour as would tend to disturb or diminish its quality. When established in a business enterprise it serves as a powerful influence increasing the efficiency and perfection of the work done as well as the satisfaction enjoyed by those who work in it.

Attention to Systems

Systems of administration, planning, operation, finance, etc., are not mere forms. They are formulations of the mind. They express a certain equilibrium which is capable of constant improvement. If one reviews the working of systems, examines the basic principles of their functioning, gives continual attention to their maintenance and perfection, they have a tendency to reveal better possibilities for innovation or greater efficiency. When not given regular attention, most systems respond by breaking down partially or completely, or some outside element comes drawing attention to the deficiency. For instance, the system of communication in a business between management and staff or between different departments may be primarily a written formal system with a regular chain of communication or an informal system of notes or oral conversation with fewer restrictions or fixed pathways. In either event if the system is ignored or violated frequently or insufficient effort made to maintain receptivity and flow of ideas, a breakdown in communication may result, leading to misunderstanding of orders, requests, information, feelings, procedures and policy, etc. Any such incident of confusion or failure of adequate communication is an indication that the system itself needs attention and perhaps improvement. Other systems such as mail distribution and response, telephone calls, cleaning, filing, accounting, transportation, food, systems of verification, referral, authorization, education, training, production lines, etc., all follow the same principle.

In any business it is a valuable exercise to periodically list all the operational systems both formal and informal, review their basic function and the procedures established to carry out that aim, and evaluate the quality of the present operation in terms of speed, economy, efficiency, accuracy, harmony, etc. Then make efforts to update and improve the system wherever possible by even a small amount.

If the atmosphere is positive, management can initiate a study of the company including employee relations, use of machines, tools and materials, operation of systems, etc. A questionnaire may be a helpful source of information from the staff. Such a study should place emphasis on the possibilities for greater progress and perfection rather than on destructive criticism of others, self-defence or justification of the *status quo*.

GARY JACOBS

5

CONSCIOUSNESS APPROACH TO BUSINESS MANAGEMENT – 2

Resources, Ideals and Harmony

The principle of full utilisation of available resources – labour, materials, energy – is a fundamental principle of modern enterprise. Wastage, loss, hoarding, careless-ness in distribution are all acts of unconsciousness, lack of attention, ignorance of the inner divinity of those things which have come to us. What is not commonly realized is that proper usage of what one has generates a momentum of flow that keeps the supply uninterrupted. At one time the manager of Mother Estates was finding it difficult to attract a sufficient labour supply for the work at hand. Despite all the usual inquiries and efforts no increase was possible. He decided to examine present usage of available labour and see if some lapse was apparent. During the meeting he found that the men had been working under poor supervision and some-times without any supervision for the past week or so and that their work output had been very low by any standards. He decided to clamp down and require a full day's work for a full day's wage. After a single day the supervisor in charge reported over a 100% increase in work completed and the very next morning three new men appeared for work unsolicited. He continued his efforts and in the following days men continued to come until there was no longer a shortage.

This principle holds good even when the required

resource is in general shortage. About the same time there was a nation-wide shortage of cement because power cuts had reduced factory production time. When the manager tried to obtain cement for building an irrigation system, the government officers told him there was a waiting list of 500 people for approximately six months. He decided to try another method. First he ordered a search of the entire garden for unused cement, anything from a handful to a bag, and gathered about three bags which he immediately used to begin the irrigation project. Then he reviewed the entire history of cement purchases and utilization at the garden and uncovered areas of wastage and misuse. He made an inner effort to arrive at the proper attitude and feelings towards the cement already used and that which was yet to come. Within three days a cousin of one of the staff called to offer 5 bags of cement at market rates. The cement was purchased and utilized. A few days later someone in town offered 15 more bags and a week later another man came forward with 50 bags which the manager purchased. Thus he could complete all the pending work.

During the power cut in 1973 there was not sufficient electricity for running the water pumps at Mother Estates. Local officials appealed to the farmers not to raise the next crop. The current supply reached a minimum of four hours per day. Even when the current was on, often the voltage was below the level required for the larger motors. Besides this there were frequent shutdowns during the four hours so that each pump had to be restarted one or more times. Furthermore, the pumps were far apart and the responsibility for starting them was given to only a few responsible men wasting additional time in travel from one pump to the next. Between all these factors 30 or 40 minutes would be lost daily before all the pumps were commissioned. The staff made a collective resolution that every minute of power must be utilized. New systems were employed to cut down on each of the sources of waste. On the first day all of the pumps were started within the first 5 minutes. Gradually the time was reduced to 15 seconds. The next day there was an announcement by the Government that 7 hours of electricity would be given. A few days later it was extended to 9 hours. Within two weeks it rose to 15 hours and finally to 20 hours during the hot season.

Besides these considerations, there is also a relationship between the availability of resources and the distribution of the final product. When the product is neglected for any reason, there may be difficulty in acquiring resources. This point is illustrated below.

II

Stagnation in the sale and distribution of the final product results from a mental inertia or hesitation on the part of management to make decisions and execute them in action. This inertia will also express itself in other places, e.g. back-up of work, delay of orders, raw material shipments, payments, etc. Often a product will accumulate in stock and, after initial efforts to move it fail, it is ignored or forgotten. The remedy lies in establishing full awareness of the product, of all possible avenues for distribution, removing hesitation and taking active initiative. When proper attention is given and all possibilities are exhausted, even when one's initiative leads only to the movement of a fraction of the quantity, life will respond by attracting buyers for the remainder.

The son of a liquor merchant came for guidance because business had been unusually slow. In the course of discussions he mentioned a $ 4000 consignment of wine that had been sitting for 6 months in the cellar without a single sale. We highlighted this unsold stock as the major cause of the business slump and requested him to examine every fact relating to the consignment from the day of purchase, to look for movements of indecisiveness, hesitation, laziness, forgetfulness, unconsciousness in his own and his father's attitude, to take a firm mental decision with genuine feeling that wine stock must be sold, to exhaust every possibility for sales and report back in two days. In short, to give the product the attention it deserved. The man returned four days later and apologized for his delay. He said that in the intervening days over half the consignment had been sold and general business had increased so much that he had no time to come earlier.

A manufacturer of hand-made paper asked us to study his factory. He said that the local supply of raw materials for the paper was in abundance but he was running into continuous delays in getting his own supplies on time. In the course of investigation we came across a stockpile of drawing paper worth $ 5000 which had been produced about a year earlier and then the order cancelled. Since then it had been lying forgotten in storage. We gave him a similar recommendation, adding that he should take initiative to remove delays from every aspect of his production lines, including delays in his response to other companies or prospective clients. The manufacturer made a firm decision to act. The next morning a truck load of raw materials arrived. But the manufacturer's hesitation remained and he failed to make a serious effort to market the paper. A few weeks later he realized his mistake and reaffirmed his decision. Within five mintues a man came in and offered to arrange the sale of the entire stock overseas. The response of life to our decisions is immediate. Accumulation of unsold stock retards the availability of raw materials, the sale of other products and the receipt of new orders.

III

In any institution, communication plays a vital role. In a dynamic organization such as a business enterprise this communication is not only composed of mental ideas and instructions, but must carry with it the enthusiasm, interest, forcefulness necessary to provoke a clear response in the recipient and motivate him to proper action. Where there is similarity of purpose, language, background, understanding and interest, words and explanations and orders are easily communicated, but where any of these are lacking, difficulties may arise.

First there may be a problem in communicating a mental idea. Even if this is accepted, it requires also a response of interest and enthusiasm to prepare the listener to act on it, and still it requires the proper receipt of instructions to know how the idea is to be implemented in practice.

For all these levels of communication, silent will can be a very effective medium. A prior condition for the effective use of silent communication is a general tuning of the different levels of the institution to the central purpose. This can be commercial in nature or psychological or spiritual. Where this tuning is present, where employees are consciously aware of the central purpose, a climate is created of receptivity and harmony in which new thought is easily introduced. Most often when a new idea or plan arises man has the tendency to speak it out immediately, to elaborate it through conversation, to test it by expression. The result is that much of the energy carried by a new inspiration or fresh thought is dissipated in premature unclarified discussion which often leads to misunderstanding, argument or initially poor response that hampers later acceptance of the finished product. Instead one can retain the fresh thought and allow it to develop quietly for some time, gradually becoming aware of the points of unclarity, weakness or possible objection. The idea is allowed to ripen and mature. One can then silently concentrate on the idea and will that others receive and accept it. One can patiently and carefully put seeds and suggestions into the atmosphere and, when the climate is right and the people receptive, give a fuller expression which will come with a far greater intensity due to the conservation and retention of energies. What commonly happens when such a procedure is followed is that either the idea is readily accepted on being presented or, even before presentation, the identical thought will be expressed by another member of the organization. This latter possibility is a very good one, for if one can suspend the egoistic need to impress others with his ideas, and allow them to accept a new thought as their own, he finds that the idea is much more readily accepted and supported.

The general climate of an organization can be made ripe for silent communication by means of periodical or regular meetings of staff. At these times emphasis can be placed on increasing the awareness of the central purpose, or introducing higher aims, or allowing open expression among the staff, all of which help to create and sustain an atmosphere of harmony, sympathy, interest, enthusiasm and participation among the members. Staff meetings have the further effect of allowing individuals and departments to become conscious of the work in all other areas of the organization and so increase their awareness of the entire institution in its dynamic wholeness. In such an atmosphere communication is made easy and it is not limited to the communication of ideas. Plans are far more effectively put into action when the person involved feels it to be his own idea or at least is given voice in the development and finalising of the procedure and a degree of discretion in the execution. Silent will can bring this about by creating a basic commonality of viewpoint and receptivity.

There are certain people who habitually respond to new ideas with a note of pessimism or by attacking and questioning them. There are others who have a vested interest in the *status quo* and resist changes or improvements in another's work. Such reactions drain the strength from a new idea, throw up a blanket of confusion and hesitation, reduce one's will and determination. In any situation where communicating a new idea is likely to meet with negativity, resistance, hostility, it is better to refrain from expression and to work inwardly until the idea has gained greater strength or the climate is more receptive. On the contrary, if one has the confidence of another person of similar disposition or close emotional identification, a certain amount of communication strengthens the movement represented by the idea and accelerates effectuation. Still moderation in speech is a valuable guideline to follow and conscious silence is a very powerful means of effectuation.

A related topic is that of gossip. In every institution there is a good measure of private conversation among staff and management concerned with the behaviour of other company members. When this conversation includes derogatory comments, sarcasm, a perverse pleasure in criticising others, it is a very powerful vibration which undermines the relationship between individuals and erodes the atmosphere of the institution. Gossip is always a negative movement which destroys harmony and goodwill. If one cannot speak positively about another or offer a mature constructive suggestion, it is better not to speak at all.

IV

We have said earlier that the institution is a living organism capable not only of expansive growth but also of rising to higher levels of functioning, a soul evolution. Like the individual, it makes such vertical upward progress when it looks up to a higher ideal and attempts to uplift its level of functioning to be in accordance with that ideal. This is Yoga. The institution has a personality determined by the purpose and circumstances of its founding, the social conditions of the time, the capacities of the founding members and all those who have since participated in its functioning. This personality is capable of a certain expansion; for instance, a business is capable of a certain growth in its volume of business which is limited by the ideal, purpose, social milieu, etc.: in short, by the institution's personality. Beyond that limit if the institution wants to expand further, it has to change its personality, it has to evolve into a higher order of institution.

Most of the principles so far discussed help to bring about a maximum growth on the horizontal level. But for growth beyond this point, the institution must consent to change itself, it must make the necessary effort of will. Horizontal expansion requires dynamic practical skills. For a vertical expansion, vision, creativity and perception are necessary.

Most business organizations are founded on an economic motive. Within this area there is still a hierarchy of levels. The proprietor can be concerned solely with his own economic security and see all his employees merely as a means to that and nothing more. This can be expanded to include concern for the economic security of the employees as well, and even further to help foster the prosperity of an industry or community or larger social group. But most institutions are moved by psychological motives as well. The founders usually have a need for creative expression, channelling of energies, the urge to adventure or new knowledge and new experiences, the learning of new skills. There is also the area of social acceptance, prestige, advancement. In these areas, too, it is possible for the institution to grow by working for the growth of these dimensions in those who work for the firm. And on a wider level the institution may begin to work towards a growth of the community. It may develop an interest in perfecting its product or service not only to increase its economic position but also for the sake of providing good service, out of a sense of social responsibility, ethics, aesthetic values. Beyond this there are even higher levels, institutions which function solely or partly for social improvement, charity, political ideals, national or international prosperity. Each time an institution gives attention to a higher level than its present functioning it takes an evolutionary step.

Established business houses often take one or more vertical steps unintentionally or unconsciously. When a firm becomes proud of its product or reputation, when it seeks to reward its employees by a fairer allotment of profits, when it takes interest in working conditions and family benefits, etc. Often such steps are taken hesitantly because they appear to be at the expense of the economic motive which has been primary. But in the history of large institutions it can be seen that this vertical growth brings with it not a loss on the economic levels but a manifold increase in profits. This is a fundamental point. When an institution rises to a higher level all the lower levels beneath receive a large expansion far beyond the limits of that lower level but in accordance with the broader potentials of a higher level.

Every institution is constantly faced with opportunities to take steps to a higher level of functioning. We start from where we are and take the next step. The resulting positive expansion then serves as an impetus for further growth so long as one does not remain satisfied with a single advance and level off there. In each part of the institution one can set an ideal a little higher than is now practised. It aids expansion of the whole. As an institution turns to a wider or higher field of life activities, the corresponding energy of that higher level uplifts the institution.

An added dimension of this principle can be seen in the evolving attitudes of the working staff. As an institution rises in ideals, the ideals and attitudes of employees will change to the degree they are identified with the institution. Where management is concerned solely with profit, employees care only for their wage share. When management shows concern for the quality of its product, employees take increased interest in the quality of work. When the firm actively gives attention to the well-being and development of its workers, the workers take a corresponding interest in the growth of the institution. When the role of the institution becomes primarily one genuine social service, the employees give service to further the institution. By so doing not only the institution evolves but the employees evolve as well as receive all the benefits of a higher level of existence.

V

Sri Aurobindo has written that all problems of nature are essentially problems of harmony. Every living organism depends on the smooth harmonious interaction and co-operation of its composite parts for growth and survival. Harmony in an institution is not limited to co-operative relations among employees or between employees and management. There is the harmony between the idea, the systems or schemes for execution and the actual outer expression. There is a harmony between principles and practice, and between understanding, acceptance and practice. For there to be a harmony there must be a tuning of the different layers of the institution to the central purpose. The ideal of harmonious relations, between parts of itself, acts as a powerful center for progress and the expansion of the entire institution. It is the universal harmony which supports all smaller conflicts. Harmony is not, as many think of it, a static or stagnant existence. It is the firm foundation of peace and stability upon which creativity, expansion and growth can flourish. Harmony brings to your service all the possibilities of the past that were missed. A general atmosphere of harmony, sympathy, good-will can be aided by not speaking critically of others, refraining from all unnecessary negative expression, particularly anger, spite and jealousy. If one forgoes negative expression even when justified, he rises to a higher level. Harmony attempted in a situation yields greater results than authority, strategy or force.

There is a harmony possible on the level of thoughts and the level of feelings; there is also a greater harmony which lies deeper in each individual, founded on the unity of all souls. If any individual in an institution makes an effort to relate to others from the deepest possible center of being, to harmonize the many divergent and conflicting elements in his own consciousness, he can release a very powerful movement of harmony in the institution as a whole. Such a movement is the most propitious condition for an expansion of the company.

VI

Every reader will surely have anticipated our attitude on movements of falsehood such as lying, deceit, misrepresentation, but the basis for this position may not be equally apparent. It is not necessary to add to the age-old debate on whether crime pays. It is certainly true that many an entrepreneur has grown wealthy by following a policy based on falsehoods of every kind. As Sri Aurobindo points out, the law of action and reaction, *karma*, is valid for each level of existence within its own domain. Lying and the like are actions on the ethical plane of mind, while business transactions are on the socio-economic plane of life. The two are not directly connected. Acts of falsehood may very well lead to economic prosperity but they also lead to moral degeneration and poverty. And since the ethical plane is a higher level of existence than the economic, the total result is a retrogression in development for the individual or institution involved. The aim of human activity is growth, progressive evolution of all the parts of the individual being and every aspect of collective life. This evolution is a movement from unconsciousness to consciousness, from ignorance and falsehood to knowledge and truth, from suffering to fulfilment. There is no possible way to further this development by a conscious act of falsehood. Moreover, though such an action may yield a material fruit, it inevitably evokes a like response from outer life. Where one has obtained business from others by misrepresentation, others will seek business from you by the same means. Where one has charged another an unreasonably high price for a product, one's own staff or suppliers or someone else will do likewise toward you. As one is to life, so life responds in one form or another.

Secrecy, concealment, hiding are conditions in which falsehood thrives. As man and his institutions develop he relies less on such means, cultivates an open and illumined climate for conducting affairs and advances more rapidly in this brighter air.

It sometimes happens that an institution is treated falsely by others even when its own attitudes and behaviour have been true. When this happens it is a good indication that the institution is on the verge of a progress to a higher level of functioning and these lower forces come to impede that movement. The only support they can ever have is from the tinge of false methods the institution sometimes permits. The solution is to fight the falsehood only by Truth. Review the past and present behaviour. Examine and correct lapses in attitudes and modes of functioning. Falsehood can never be fought by falsehood.

A nationally known firm in the U.S. was awarded a large contract by one of the State Governments. The official in-charge said the only condition was that the consultant must demand an extra large fee and hand over the excess to him. The consultant refused the illegal proposition and lost the job. Some years later under a new government administration the same consulting firm was awarded the largest consulting contract the state had ever issued. This time it was all legal.

One's own latent capacity for falsehood, slander, ill-will and jealousy, even when unexpressed, leaves one open to over negativity from others. The best protection is a sincere examination of the roots of such vibrations within oneself.

GARY JACOBS

6

CONSCIOUSNESS APPROACH TO BUSINESS MANAGEMENT – 3

Responsibility, Powers and Freedom

Sri Aurobindo writes that "Freedom is the highest law and the last consummation". To the extent that an individual is committed to the central aims of an institution and identified with it, he should be given freedom to err as well as succeed, for only so can he and the institution grow. Man responds to pressure, force, commands and outer discipline by a behavioural conformity which tends to revert to old forms as soon as the pressure is removed. It is only under conditions of freedom that man will impose discipline upon himself and only self-discipline, meaning a true consent of the will, can create true personality growth.

To put it another way, to the extent that a man shows the capacity to exercise freedom in a disciplined manner without letting it fall into licentiousness, he must be given room to exercise his free choice. Each man will have strong areas where freedom can be given and here he should be given free scope. The very act of giving freedom to a man in a new area serves as an incentive for him to extend his trust-worthiness to other areas. One should look for this development and encourage it.

Yet the freedom one gives should not become an occasion for another to exploit you. It is as wrong from the higher point of view to allow oneself to be exploited as to exploit others. The fact is that when freedom is given man almost always utilizes it both for constructive growth and for greater self-indulgence – the two are distinct yet usually go together. To give freedom to others requires that one is himself established in that freedom inwardly, possessing a great inner stability, strength, patience and will for man's growth. If these qualities are not there in some measure it is better to proceed cautiously, otherwise an initial gesture of freedom to others will be followed by a rapid withdrawal of the same and may lead to a demoralised atmosphere in which the individual takes less interest or initiative than ever. Some degree of misuse or exploitation will always be there and is tolerable. It is the price paid for the truest and most rapid growth of oneself, those around and the institution as a whole. Freedom implies and complements responsibility. If freedom is given it should eventually result in evolving a greater sense of and capacity for accepting responsibility on the part of the entrusted individual. As these grow, the man and the institution flourish.

In institutional life freedom and responsibility express themselves as an attitude of professionalism. Management implicitly recognizes the qualifications, competence, maturity and capacity of each man to properly exercise a certain degree of freedom and responsibility in a constructive manner. To relate to another as a professional is essentially a gesture of respect for his capabilities. Yet the true basis for respect is not training or experience. It is founded on the essential divinity and dignity which is common to all human beings and the capacity of every man to develop his personality and

capabilities further by the unfolding of the hidden
potentialities within him. Every man merits a certain
degree of respect and possesses a certain capacity for
responsible activity. If one relates to the essential core of
divinity in a man, he responds by bringing forward his
best qualities and properly utilizing the freedom and
responsibility given him.

II

Individuals and institutions make decisions on many
levels according to many standards of conduct, ranging
from motives of pure self-interest, social custom, legal
right, moral and ethical right, to spiritual or inner right.
At times a business may be faced with a situation in
which what is permitted by law does not coincide with
what is really fair to the party concerned. For example,
law may establish a certain minimum wage for
labourers, yet the work required does not truly fall in the
normal labour category and one has the prerogative to
pay by the law. By ignoring the legal standard and acting
according to a more just guideline, one raises the level of
the institution and fosters its growth. In fact, each time
an individual or an institution acts according to a higher
standard than that which the situation necessitates, he
makes a growth in consciousness.

An industrialist was plagued with complete shutdown
of his three factories due to a labour strike. The trouble
had been instigated by a single man who became leader
of the workers and made untenable demands on their
behalf. After more than two months this leader was

caught in possession of a stolen watch belonging to one of the supervisors. The police placed him in jail. The industrialist knew of this principle for the exercise of power and wanted to rely on the justness of his position rather than on legal power. After great hesitation he decided not to press charges and ordered the police to release the man. The leader-thief came directly to the industrialist. He apologized for his behaviour, requested the workers to accept the fair terms offered and abandon their strike, and then he promptly left the company and the city.

The greatest power available to a man is his highest ideal or his deepest faith – that is the Divine for him. Let his ultimate reliance be on these. Then lower authorities such as law can be resorted to when necessary as an instrument for this power to express itself.

III

Exhaust your resources and life will respond.

Often it happens that in one or more areas of a project a bottleneck is reached and progress grinds to a halt. It may be a need for new ideas, new informations, more men, money, materials, etc. At these times it is good to step back from the particular issue at hand and examine the overall functioning of the institution in the light of the principles already described. One may observe how far the operating principles have strayed from the basic ideals of the institution, how adequately attention has been given to the different elements of the work, what areas lack or have lost a basic harmony of functioning, and so on.

After such an investigation has been carried out and corrections been implemented, it may still be that the particular problem at hand needs an added impetus to get it moving. Where the atmosphere surrounding the work is favourable, where disharmony continues to prevail, it is better to patiently refrain from action until the mood changes. But where the atmosphere is good and all elements seem ready for a breakthrough, then it may be that a token effort will turn the corner and bring success. This means to make a determined initiation and persistent endeavour to no matter how small an extent it may be possible, and do whatever can be done in the given circumstances, exhaust all possibilities, potentials and resources. At the point where one has fully exhausted his energies and capacities, life responds by bringing the components necessary to complete the work. Where human effort is exhausted, one opens to the forces of universal life which take up the movement. But if one stops at the penultimate step, there is no response.

IV

In the process of making institutional decisions one is constantly faced not only with two or more alternatives, but the opportunity to act out of a higher set of values. When one chooses the higher, it leads to growth and incidentally includes the possible benefit of the lower.

A few examples are given of priorities which help the institution to expand:

> Long term over short term
> Progress over profit

Convention over convenience
Effort over comfort
Sublimation over diversion
Resolution into a harmony over solution
Institution's welfare over department's welfare
Employee's utility over management utility
Confrontation over appeasement
Compromise at a higher level over confrontation.

GARY JACOBS

7

CONSCIOUSNESS APPROACH TO BUSINESS MANAGEMENT – IV

Money, Motivation & Progress

What has been said regarding animate and inanimate objects is equally true of money. It responds to attention. Keeping an exact account of what is spent is one form of attention which promotes a non-stop flow of funds for work. The principle of total and proper utilization also applies. It can be seen that when one is left with a few more dollars and further finance is not forthcoming, the incoming money flow awaits the spending of the last cent. If money has been improperly expended on a certain item and efforts are taken to reverse the previous act, before long further sources of funds are revealed.

But money is not merely an object. Rather the material currency employed "...is the visible sign of a universal force, and this force in its manifestation on earth works on the vital and physical planes and is indispensable to the fullness of the outer life. In its origin and its true action it belongs to the Divine" (Sri Aurobindo, *The Mother*). "...money is not meant to make money....

Money is meant to increase the wealth, the prosperity and the productiveness of a group, a country or, better, of the whole earth. Money is a means, a force, a power, and not an end in itself. And like all forces and all powers, it is by movement and circulation that it grows and increases its power, not by accumulation and stagnation" (The Mother). The normal human consciousness fails to see the Divine in money, and it wants to possess it for its value in fulfilling desires and the self-gratification of man's ego. Money is a form of the Divine in manifestation and it has a higher role to play in the life of each individual and the collectivity.

A business institution is based primarily on the motivation of economic self-interest directly in competition with others. Yet one can see in a larger view that, through this competition, not only a single business and its employees but the economy as a whole grows and prospers. The principle of competition is true at one level. But a higher truth is that of association, mutual interchange and collective progress. Wealth is not a fixed quantity in the world to be fought over. It is an ever expanding movement of prosperity fostered by the creative activity of institutions. In the long run a successful institution is only possible in a strong economy where others also prosper and the individual success adds to the collective prosperity.

When a business institution recognizes this interdependence between all elements of the economy and chooses for its motivation and practical philosophy the development and prosperity of the economy as a whole, it oversteps the narrow bounds of competitive self-interest and rises to a higher level of idealism. All its decisions, policies, actions have a broader perspective and a sounder basis. The result is that, having renounced the primary emphasis on its own survival, it becomes an essential component of the larger economic system. Life responds through the entire system to ensure that the company survives and prospers. In its activity the company becomes a broad channel for the flow of prosperity into the system. It attracts wealth to itself, and freely distributes it to the rest, far more than was possible by its narrower pursuit.

For an individual or an institution, the true attitude towards money is neither a greed to possess it for oneself nor an active distaste for wealth or the activities which create it. Money is a power of the Divine to be utilized for the development and prosperity of every man, institution, country, all mankind.

II

This subject has already been discussed in terms of the institution as a whole and its governing ideal. The same holds true for every smaller unit of the company down to the individual. Simply stated, the principle is that the higher, less selfish, personal and egoistic one's motivation, the more he grows, and the more he receives. On the lower levels man is motivated by a desire for reward — money, fame, prestige, respect, success. At a higher level he works out of interest. Interest is a broader, less personal, more mental motive than desire. By choosing it one does not necessarily sacrifice the lower rewards but adds to them the satisfaction which comes from following one's interest. The highest level of motivation is service to another, to the firm, community, society, mankind, the Divine. Service brings with it the pure joy of self-giving and in the process life sees to it that one's desires and interests are also fulfilled. The basis of service is a decision to give of oneself. It is man's highest motive for action and it is the key to life. The principle of giving can be applied at all levels. One can give wealth and material possessions, give interest or attention, sympathy, psychological support, etc. When the management of an institution is able to practise this in its relationship with employees, other institutions and the society at large, then it opens the way for an unlimited growth, expansion and prosperity.

III

Progress is normally thought of as the end result, the goal of all one's efforts, not something that can itself be practised as a principle. But it need not be so, if one makes progress the governing ideal of all work and at every moment chooses it in favour of any other alternative. Progress means a constant effort to upgrade one's ideas, services, employees and systems. One may strive for the progress not only of the institution but of all its members, of all other institutions, of the larger society of which they are a part. To do this one must remember in every situation that the important thing is progress. No single job, no opportunity for quick profit should move him to waver from this principle.

The key to progress can be found in the Mother's statement that one must always strive for perfection and that the particular level of perfection attainable today does not matter so long as one reaches at least one step higher tomorrow. Life never stands still. If we do not progress we regress. The best way to start is by a period of sincere self-observation. Examine the entire institution as a whole and in all its parts and let each man examine himself also. Then whatever the result one must be objective and not criticize or condemn himself or others, only let one know what he is. Then take the decision that tomorrow each aspect or as many aspects as possible must be upgraded one step. It is helpful to keep a journal of one's observations and to then put in writing a plan for progress in the coming day and week. The programme must not be just a glimmering ideal one would like to attain. Then that small step should be implemented. This can be done on a group basis for the entire organisation or each department but it can also be done by every individual working member. Daily each man can decide to take one step towards greater perfection in work, a step which he can take himself independent of the behaviour of others. Let him daily take new steps while maintaining all the perfection attained in previous days. This maintaining of what has been previously accomplished is essential.

What one achieves in himself he has the power to pass on to others only after he has gained complete mastery of it. There is an age-old principle, "Practise what you preach". Better than this, practise to perfection and communicate that perfection to others by a silent will and a living example. In this light, every job is an opportunity for progress. If one concentrates on growth, expansion and rising to higher levels of motivation, one creates an atmosphere which attracts success, prosperity and new opportunity. It is not necessary to share these thoughts with others in the institution if there is any resistance to them. All that one has to do if he accepts them is to work silently along these lines, exhausting his personal and official capacities. His responsibility ends there. Where he ends, life will take over.

IV

The basis of the Consciousness Approach is the corres-pondence between man's inner consciousness and events in outer life. Man is normally aware only of physical needs, life impulses, feelings and thoughts. Therefore the outer life of most men is a response to the quality of these inner elements. By changing the inner condition, one brings about a responsive change in the external world.

But consciousness is not limited to this. Behind the surface personality in man lies his true inner being. By contacting this deeper center he gains freedom from all the conflicting elements of his personality and the power to mould them into a unified harmonious whole. He discovers the Divine within himself. So too, behind and within all other living beings and material objects, there is a center of pure consciousness. By entering into conscious relationship with that center in other things and beings he gains a direct knowledge of his external environment and the power to influence conditions and events. He discovers the Divine in the world and in life.

In this truer perspective the term Consciousness Approach means that all the problems of life, rather all items of life, positive and negative, are referred to one center in man, i.e. his deepest inner consciousness. That should be the only center of reference. The usual standards of behaviour, viz. mental understanding, ethical norms, social expectations, are for this purpose discarded. Therefore the method is applicable only in so far as one places total reliance on the inner conscious-ness to the exclusion of normal methods of life. By an inner mastery it is possible to control all outer events.

There has been no attempt here to construct a new system of business management. Systems are mental. Rather it is to evoke a response in the reader to the existence of a deeper center of functioning in man from which all the problems which perpetually confront life and mind can be effectively resolved in a higher order. The detailed discussion of principles is intended to stimulate the mind to seek this deeper center. This center, the true being in man, is the source of unlimited consciousness which can be channeled into creativity on any plane of existence. Yet the greater achievement is to forego the utilization of this consciousness for one's own ends and instead become a conscious personality through which it can flow in effectuating its own creative intention. That intention is nothing less than the progressive evolution of the individual and the human collectivity towards a life of greater knowledge, love, power and beauty.

GARY JACOBS

8

THE PHILOSOPHY OF MANAGEMENT

The East and the West

In the pre-war years, India learned the technique of modern management mostly from the United Kingdom. In the post-war years, India turned to the United States in this and many other spheres of knowledge and techniques. Now we are learning it from many other nations as well. As we are entering deeper and deeper, year by year, into the processes of modern industrialization, the subject of management is assuming increasing importance. We are facing the problems of tackling efficiently the organization and management of our ever-expanding developmental monetary investments, of our vast material resources, and of our ever-expanding work-force belonging to the entire spectrum of men and women at work in our offices, factories, workshops, and educational, hospital, and other service institutions. There is a quick transition taking place in our expanding industry from hereditary to professional management cadres; this has called for the need for management training, for the fulfilment of which more and more institutes and schools of management training are coming up in all parts of our country.

One salutary development in this field, discernible during the past few years, is the interest in, what is called, the philosophy of management, on the one hand, and in the question whether India has any philosophy of her own on the subject of management, on the other.

Every nation, every culture, has its own approach to the subject of management, as well as to other forms of group life and activity. Today, there are two great nations which are highly specialized in the field of management and have their own philosophies relating to it: one is America and the other is Japan. Many in India do not know that their own country also has its own philosophy of administration and management; but today it is a hopeful sign that many of our people are eager to know it; and I have come across books by various Indian writers expounding this subject, basing their treatment on the great Yoga philosophy and technique of the *Bhagavadgita*.

This new interest in India's own philosophy and approach is stimulated by our people's witnessing, during the post-war years, the amazing phenomenon of the management philosophy and techniques of an Occidental or Western Country like America, which have been dominating the whole world for many decades, now yielding to the management philosophy and techniques of an Oriental or Eastern country like Japan. We are now witnessing the publication of a plethora of books on management by American writers, comparing the two management systems and praising the Japanese system as more efficient. I wish to draw your attention to one such book which, in content and style, makes fascinating reading: *The Art of Japanese Management* by Richard Tanner Pascale and Anthony G. Athos; its front title cover carries this comment of *The Washington Post* 'If there is one major lesson to be learned from the Japanese business structure, it is how to manage'. The 'Introduction' to the book by the Managing Director of a reputed American company has this to say about the deficiencies of the American system:

> This is an important book; its importance derives from both its timing and its contents. We are, I believe, at the beginning of a period where significant new research into the practice of management is essential. The Academic journals, the business press, and the popular media, have all recently speculated on the managerial causes of weak competitive performance by American enterprise. Top managements, the business schools that train them, and the consultants who advise them, have all been faulted for a destructive preoccupation with analytical technique – too narrow in its conception and too short-term in its application....
>
> The weaknesses in American management that have been at fault in our declining international competitiveness have not been so much an over-reliance on analysis and technique, as a failure to fit the application of technique into a broader, more complete, and more coherent concept of what enables organizations to perform in a superior way and to endure over time. The authors present such a concept, called "the 7-S Model".

The 7-S model is later presented by the authors as: Strategy, Structure, Systems, Staff, Style, Skill, with Superordinate goals inserted between the first three mechanical items and the last three human items. By superordinate goals, the Japanese mean the shared values and goals that bind together the fabric of all successful enduring corporations. They constitute the *dharma*, the corpus of spiritual values, of any human group. The 'Introduction' further states:

> In describing the 7-S model, Pascale and Athos do not disparage the analytical methodologies that have been developed, taught, and applied during the three decades. These methods have contributed importantly to the formulation of business strategies, the development of effective organization structures, and the definition of useful systems for managing businesses – large and small. About this there is no doubt. But the authors present a framework of management that blends thinking about style, skills, staff and superordinate goals, with notions of strategy, structure and systems into an interdependent reinforcing network. It is the absence of, or conflicts within this complete network, the authors argue, that accounts for weak corporate performance. This point is made and illustrated with numerous examples and comparisons between Japanese and American management practices.

The authors state at the beginning of their book[1] that 'man is limited not so much by his tools as by his vision'. They continue:

> The principal objectives of this book can be stated simply.
> First, regardless of society or culture, mankind

has discovered only a limited number of tools for making organizations work...

Second, managerial reality is not an absolute; rather, it is socially and culturally determined...

Third, firms which perform well year after year, whether Japanese or American, tend to have a lot in common...

Let us briefly consider how we got where we are...

The Industrial Revolution, with its invention of mass production, diminished the importance of the skilled trades and the social affiliations obtained through them. The emergence of the concept of "factors of production" (land, labour and capital) had revolutionary implications for the Western view of humankind. Humans (the labour content) were no longer an inextricable part of the organic whole of society. Rather, the person, as labourer, became an objectified and standardized component of the production process. Not surprisingly, this view of "labour" tended to divorce man as a social and spiritual being from his "productive" role at work. Correspondingly this reaffirmed the lingering lesson of the centuries that one's spiritual and social life should reside outside the work-place. This concept has persisted in Western thinking to this day and, as we will see, it is one of the sources of our present problem...

The principal difference between Eastern Institutions and those in the West is that ours is turned to organizational structure and formal systems to cope with these challenges. In contrast, Eastern institutions, while until recently advancing more slowly in thinking about organizational forms and formal systems, paid much more attention to social and spiritual means....

Eastern societies were so populous, and because spiritual, public, and private matters were so integrated, their organizations tended to regard the task of control in the context of the whole of human needs, rather than as a more narrow transaction between labour and capital. They were generally more sophisticated than the West in utilizing social and spiritual forces for the organization's benefit, and in accepting the responsibilities to their employees that went with such broad influence.

While discussing the successful managerial philosophy and practices of one of the Japanese companies, the Matsushita Electric Company, the authors introduce a whole section entitled: 'Spiritual Values'[2]:

"Spiritual" is an unlikely term in a narrative of corporate life. Yet nothing less suffices to capture the strong belief system that underlies Matsushita's philosophy...

The Matsushita philosophy provides a basis of meaning beyond the products it produces. Matsushita was the first company in Japan to have a song and a code of values. "It seems silly to Westerners", says one executive, "but every morning at 8 a.m. all across Japan, there are 87, 000 people reciting the code of values and singing together. It's like we are all a community". Matsushita foresaw that a life-time's organizational experience shapes one's character indelibly. It was unthinkable, in his view, that work, which occupies at least half of our waking hours, should be denied its powerful role. The firm, therefore, had an inescapable responsibility to help the employees' inner selves. This responsibility could best be realized by tying the corporation to society and the individual, by insisting that management serves as trainers and developers of character, not just as exploiters of human resources.

Some Western minds will find these ideas at best remote, at worst delusive. But such a connection between philosophy and hard-headed business objectives is one that the Japanese take as natural. One observer notes that Matsushita provides two distinct kinds of training. One is basic skills training, but the second and more fundamental one is training in Matsushita values. These values are inculcated through a long apprenticeship across one's career. The newly hired are exposed to them continually. As a member of any working group, each person is asked at least once every month, to give a ten minute talk to his group on the firm's values and its relationship to society. It is said that nothing is so powerful in persuading oneself as having to persuade others....

The basic principles, beliefs, and values of the firm are as follows:

Basic Business Principles

To recognize our responsibilities as industrialists, to foster progress to promote the general welfare of society, and to devote ourselves to the further development of world-culture.

Employee's Creed

Progress and development can be realized only through the combined efforts and co-operation of each member of our Company. Each of us, therefore, shall keep this idea constantly in mind, as we devote ourselves to the continuous improvement of our Company.

The Seven "Spiritual" Values

1. National Service through Industry
2. Fairness
3. Harmony and Co-operation
4. Struggle for Betterment
5. Courtesy and Humility
6. Adjustment and Assimilation
7. Gratitude

These values, taken to heart, provide a spiritual fabric of great importance....

The Director of a major Matsushita subsidiary comments:

Matsushita's management philosophy is very important to us. It enables us to match Western efficiency without being one bit less Japanese. Perhaps the ultimate triumph of Matsushita is the balancing of the rationalism of the West with the spiritualism of the East.

Referring to the need for all managements to deal differently with human resources from material resources, organisation and style, the authors say[3]:

> The inherent preferences of organizations are clarity, certainty, and perfection. The inherent nature of human relationships involves ambiguity, uncertainty, and imperfection. How one honours, balances and integrates the needs of both is the real trick of management.

I had expounded the science of spiritual growth from individuality, *vyaktitva*, to personality, *vikasita vyaktitva*, as understood in Vedanta. Sri Ramakrishna (1836-1886) calls it the growth of *kāncā āmi*, 'unripe "I"', into *pākā āmi*, 'ripe "I"'. Individuality, or *kāncā āmi*, is compared by Bertrand Russell to a billiard ball whose relation to another billiard ball is only coexistence or collision. But men must learn to enter into each other and work in harmony with each other, in co-operation and team spirit. This is achieved by the spiritual growth from individuality to personality from *kāncā āmi* to *pākā āmi*. This is based on the Advaitic vision of a basic spiritual unity. Western outlook is dominated by the logical dualism and contradiction introduced by Aristotle and Descartes. Expounding the difference between this dualistic Western and monistic Far Eastern (and also Indian) views of 'self' and 'individuality', the authors state[4]:

> There are few concepts as deeply embedded in the Western mind as the concept of "self". Our philosophy, language, and psychology are filled with it.

We see our "Selves" as distinct entities, separate from all others in most important respects, with separate beliefs, talents, and experiences. In Japan, each person is believed to possess a unique spirit, soul, mind, and heart – but his self (or "self-concept") is seen as an impediment to growth. People are regarded less as individuals than as collaborators in the context of their roles. One's separate "identity" is not singled out as the primary sign of personal development throughout the life cycle, as it is in the West....

The Japanese perceive the drawing of lines between self and "others" as arbitrary. Their culture emphasizes reciprocal influences; ours tend to empahsize separateness. Westerners struggle to develop and then retain separate identity in the face of invading influences. The Japanese tend to develop an "inclusive identity" that incorporates those close to them....

For cultural reasons, dependence is a disquieting word for Westerners; for practical reasons, excessive independence is too.... What is needed, conceptually, is a clearer notion of interdependence that permits us to preserve the best of independence and dependence without getting the worst of both. The Japanese accomplish this through the concept of Wa. Technically, Wa means group harmony. But its full meaning encompasses a range of English words – unity, cohesiveness, team-spirit.

Highlighting the importance of the current change

from the concept of 'Personnel Management' to the concept of 'Human Resource Management', the authors remark[5]:

> What is needed in the West is a non-deified, non-religious "spiritualism" that enables a firm's superordinate goals to respond truly to the inner meanings that many people seek in their work – or, alternatively, seek in their lives and could find at work, if only that were more culturally acceptable.

> Western institutions are, in fact, backing into this role. Two forces are at work: employees seeking more meaning for their jobs and demanding more concern from the corporation, and legislative pressures enforcing a broad range of personal services, including employee rights to counselling. In response to these forces, most major firms now describe these activities as 'Human Resource Management' instead of 'Personnel' – it is to be hoped, the first step in adopting a larger perspective.

In the concluding chapter, the authors speak of American national culture, and American industrial management subculture, as the two root causes of America's recent management decline. Comparing this with the Japanese management philosophy and techniques, the authors conclude[6]:

> What we saw was that generally we were very similar to the Japanese on all the "hard-ball" strategy, structure, and systems. Our major diffe-

rences are in the "soft-ball" S's – skills, styles, staff and superordinate goals. Their culture gives them advantages in the "softer" S's, because of its approach to ambiguity, uncertainty, and imperfection, and to interdependence as the most approved mode of relationship. We saw that their development of language and forms of discourse, especially their indirection, permit high development of skills we seldom achieve or honour. Their careful attention to their human resources, from the initial recruitment all the way through retirement, made us look as wasteful of our people, as we have been of our other resources. We saw how the boss-subordinate relationship encourages a degree of effective collaboration that we might envy, and how consensus is used to accomplish smooth implementation, which often eludes us. In short, we saw that, by comparison, we were all too often grossly underdeveloped in our sophistication about "man-in organization", and powerfully disadvantaged by our culture.

The authors warn, in the last but one sentence of their book, that 'the task is not to imitate cosmetically, but to evolve organically'.

Lessons to India

All aspects of management and administration in India, including our relevant training institutions, will do well to sit back calmly and ponder over what the philosophy and technique of Japanese management mean to us. As

Eastern countries, both have a common spiritual background. We should remember the Zen meditation, which gave Japan trained and disciplined minds, is an Indian contribution which India herself, in recent centuries, failed to utilize and profit from; we depended solely on an amalgam of rituals and ceremonies, magic and miracles, and superstition in religion, and the stuffing of minds in education, neglecting the vital discipline of training of the mind in both. A little thinking will reveal to us the close kinship of the Japanese philosophy and technique to our own philosophy and value-system. This revelation will impart a dynamism and direction to our administration and management, now sadly lacking, when a good percentage of our people grasp it and become inspired by it. They will then realize the implications of certain truths that stare at us. Whereas Japan has very few natural resources, our country has plenty of them; in intelligence and ability also, we are not below the Japanese or Americans. Yet, both of them are far ahead of us in economic and social development. We are still an undeveloped and developing nation, even after 40 years of political freedom, economic planning, and crores of investment.

Thinking over these facts, it will become obvious to us that some vital element is lacking in us. That vital element is trained and disciplined and socially oriented minds and hearts. Commenting on the statement of Shri Krishna at the commencement of chapter four of the Gita, that the great philosophy of a dynamic and comprehensive spirituality called Yoga, expounded by him in chapters two and three, became gradually diluted and lost – *yogo naṣṭaḥ parantapa*.... Sankaracarya elucidates that 'it was lost when it fell into the hands of weaklings and people bereft of disciplined and trained minds and hearts': *durbalān ajitendriyān prāpya*. If and when that long missing element is supplied, our nation can, not only reach the level of the Japanese economic and social performance, but even out-reach it. It is on this vital missing link that we have to concentrate our national attention, and identify and introduce it into our education, religion, and inter-human situations.

The first thing that will strike us then will be the discovery that many of our people have no knowledge of their own philosophy of life and work, and that we have been and are imitating cosmetically Western philosophy and methods, and not evolving organically our own, on the basis of our own philosophy and culture. That makes our actions *ad hoc*, and under the tyranny of the immediate present. Most of our people know only the weak and ugly aspects, the popular *deśācāra* and *lokācāra* aspects, of their country's culture and religion; and these are obsolete and irrelevant in the modern age. This limited understanding has made them bereft of self-respect, and apologetic, which weakens their national resolve and capacity to seek and assimilate the real philosophical and spiritual elements of their own culture and, in that strength, to seek and assimilate the best aspects of Western and other cultures, and not merely imitate their cheap elements.

But when our people will slowly grasp the Advaitic vision, the vision of oneness, of non-separateness and assimilate the dynamic philosophy of calm, silent, co-operative work as taught in our Bhagavad-Gita – the attitude referred to in the third chapter entitled Karma Yoga: *parasparam bhāvayantaḥ śreyaḥ param avapsyatha*, 'by mutuality and co-operation, all shall achieve the highest welfare' – and learn to respect the dignity and inherent worth of oneself and others as sparks of the One Divine Atman, we shall capture a high level of self-discipline, human concern, and practical efficiency. And these basic human transformations will invest all aspects of our administration and management with tremendous dynamism and humanistic orientation. All management and administration derive from the prevailing social attitudes and outlook; and our present attitudes and outlook are not conducive to efficient management.

A nation cannot become great without self-discipline; and self-discipline is the mark of a free man, as indiscipline is the mark of a slave. That we are still a highly indisciplined people, and also riddled with petty jealousies, only show that we have not shed our slave mentality, though external political freedom has come to us. Unfree India had more free people than free India has. This tragedy is the result of not using that freedom, which came to us after centuries of political slavery and social humiliation, to energetically work to transform Indian society from an undeveloped to a highly developed one. Our people used their undoubtedly high intelligence only to advance themselves, in total neglect of the nation; they forgot that such lives are empty, in spite of high or low levels of money or power, that such people are more dead than alive. One hope-inspiring sign on the horizon of our nation, since the last four or five years, is that this truth of what constitutes human worth and human excellence is dawning on increasing numbers of our people. This must lead us to a 'Discovery of India' as Jawaharlal Nehru termed it in his own case, and making that discovery flow into an energetic effort to the reshaping of India in the modern age in the light of her lofty philosophy and spirituality and rich culture.

Efficiency of administration and management depends as much on the quality of the employees as on that of the administrative heads and managers and executives. If our people as a whole are imbued with self-respect, a sense of honour, self-discipline, and citizenship virtues, and all our managers and employees are drawn from that common citizen pool of the nation, the entire administration and management techniques and processes will undergo a revolutionary transformation in India; it will become an efficient science and art of drawing out the best from oneself and from others in a dynamic effort at total human development, growth and fulfilment. That will transform our country from being merely the largest democracy, in view of our mere population strength, into the greatest democracy, in view of our people getting endowed with keen minds, and large hearts, and efficient hands.

Unfree people, like immature children, are difficult to manage; but free and responsible people are easy to manage. All management involves commanding and obeying. But, in a democracy, all commanding should avoid injuring the self-respect of the one commanded, and all obeying should be on the basis of one's freedom and self-respect, and never degrade into cringing. It is only in this context that inter-human relationships in the management situation can evoke the best from the other person. Such free and responsible people will be naturally endowed with the citizenship virtues and graces of duty and punctuality, co-operation and commitment. Such employees will not need even supervision of their work, for supervision militates against a person's sense of honour, and all truly free and responsible people are always endowed with this great virtue of personal honour and self-respect. Our employees, in a majority of cases, are still far away from these virtues, in spite of their being free citizens of a free nation. They lack the virtues of duty and punctuality, because they lack a sense of true freedom and personal honour.

It is educative to know how employees of other free nations behave with a sense of human values and social responsibility, and how they look at our ways. Here are two such illustrations:

When I was the Secretary of the Ramakrishna Mission Institute of Culture, Calcutta, twenty years ago, we had a British citizen as a manager of our International Scholars and Guest Houses. One day, she came up to me in joy and said that she had received a letter from the British Government in London, stating that she had just become eligible to receive her old-age pension according to the relevant British law, and enclosing the first cheque of that pension. She herself had no idea of her eligibility for that pension; but the staff in the relevant British Government office in far away London had kept track of her case and given her, her due, without her having to ask for it! Here we can see the living touch of human values in administration. What a contrast in our own country! Here, thousands of persons in her position not only will not get their dues spontaneously and in time from the government and other service institutions, but they will fail to get them even after knocking about from office to office for months and years! What a distance our management and administration have to travel from the current callousness and human uncon- cern to spontaneous human responses to human situa- tion! This is the elementary spiritual growth as respon- sible citizens that man has to achieve in our country in a big and pervasive way; and I am sure that before this century is out, our people will achieve that growth, which is the fruit of true education and true religion in one.

A recent Japanese visitor to our country was struck by seeing the widespread wearing of wrist watches by our people, including even our clerks, rickshaw-pullers, and other low-paid citizens. He remarked to his Indian friend. In spite of Japan being more economically advanced than India, we Japanese do not consume most of what our industry produces like wrist watches and clocks, but largely export them for strengthening our economy; and what strikes me further in India is that everyone here wears a watch, but nobody is punctual, that the watch seems to be more a status symbol than a useful instrument of punctuality!

As a first step to toning up management and instilling a measure of self-discipline in all employees, and putting them on the road leading to the qualitative enrichment it is worth while to consider introduction of a programme of commencing the day's work in all institutions with all the staff, from manager to the peon, sitting together, or in small groups, in silent meditation for five to ten minutes. With the mind dwelling on God as the one Self in all beings, and with the thought of dedicating one's life and work to that reality through devoted service to all beings in the chosen field of one's work.

Following our own philosophy, science and art of management and administration, we have to build up the manhood and womanhood of our vast nation and render our distinctive service to the rest of the world. And the world is waiting for it. By 2000 A.D., we have to work unitedly to make India a great world power, but a world power with a unique historically acquired character of her own, namely, a power for diffusion of spiritual and human values, a power for international peace, co-operation, and welfare. In her long history of over five thousand years, when often she had developed mighty empires with economic and military strength, India has maintained uniformly peaceful international relations, without any instance of military aggression on other nations. But she has, silently and effectively invaded the hearts and minds of other nations, in her own way, namely, through inspiring ideas and ideals and great spiritual personalities like Buddha, for which she became an international legend of wisdom, and humanism.

SWAMI RANGANATHANANDA

References:

1. *The Art of Japanese Management* by Richard Tanner Pascale E. Anthony G. Athos, pp. 22-25.
2. *Ibid.*, pp. 49-52.
3. *Ibid.*, p. 105.
4. *Ibid.*, pp. 121-25.
5. *Ibid.*, p. 193.
6. *Ibid.*, p. 204.

9

HUMAN VALUES IN MANAGEMENT

The purpose of science, as expounded by Thomas Huxley, the collaborator of Charles Darwin in the nineteenth century, was not only the advancement of knowledge, but also the 'alleviation of human suffering'. If the first is to lead to the second, there is need to wed the pursuit of knowledge, i.e. education with the humanistic impulse. Unfortunately, after independence, India divorced her education, politics, and administration from this humanistic impulse; so these lost the capacity to alleviate human suffering; some of these, especially politics, developed, on the other hand, even the capacity to aggravate human suffering, by infecting and distorting our education, administration, and labour movement. So, along with human unconcern, and always as a result of it, we witness the spiralling of social evils like bribery, corruption, tax evasion, smuggling, lack of citizenship virtues like duty, punctuality, honest work for the remuneration one gets, and public spirit. The types, varieties, and range of social malpractices that our people indulge in today are unprecedented, not only in our own history, but in all human history. Along with the physical malnutrition of our millions, the spiritual malnutrition of the educated and well-fed classes of our nation today is writ large in every field of our national activity.

Swami Vivekananda's luminous man-making and nation-building ideas and ideals contain the much-needed spiritual nourishment for our people today.

Here are two sentences from his letters, which have reference to our education, and to our dignity as citizens of free India, respectively. Says he in a letter addressed from Chicago to his dynamic and dedicated young disciple in Madras, Alasinga Perumal, in 1894[1]:

> My heart is too full to express my feeling – you know it; you can imagine it. So long as the millions live in hunger and ignorance, I hold every man a traitor who, having been educated at their expense, pays not the least heed to them!

Again, in a letter written to the Maharaja of Mysore on 23rd June 1894, he says[2]:

> This life is short, the vanities of the world are transient, but they alone live who live for others, the rest are more dead than alive.

He awakened our long dormant national energies and impressed on them this humanistic touch. During our immediate feudal past, there was very little of this human orientation; it was often anti-human, with caste-exclusiveness, untouchability, and human exploitation as its outstanding characteristics. Our upper classes missed the great opportunity then to educate and raise our common people and build up a great nation; not only did they fail to do this, but they also sat heavily on the common people and fattened themselves, by doing which they brought themselves and the common people under the shame of foreign domination and humiliation for centuries. In spite of this unhappy experience of the immediate past, how did our educated classes slide quickly from the ecstasy of freedom of our independence day on 15th August 1947 to rank selfishness, human unconcern, and complacency thereafter? Many of our educated countrymen today are 'dead' people because they live for themselves and have forgotten to live for others, forgotten to live and work for the nation. Having got educated at the cost of the nation he or she has forgotten the nation, neglected to serve it and raise the rest of the people; they have thus become traitors to the nation. Vivekananda will teach all such people in our nation today how to live, in the true sense of the term, by living for others, and how to cease to be traitors to the nation, by serving the common people with their knowledge and talents. He will inject this much-needed human motivation into their actions and thoughts.

II

Selfishness and self-centredness, and the evils flowing from them, have resulted in nobody being happy or satisfied in our country. Our people are to take all steps to reverse this downward trend and work hard to dispel the current dismal atmosphere and make every one happy and fulfilled. This is done by participating in the nation-building process, instead of remaining a self-centred looker-on. Our intelligentsia must be possessed with this central passion: 'This is our nation; these are our people; we must do whatever we can to develop the manhood and womanhood of our vast population'. We have to take the preamble of our Constitution seriously and work devotedly to ensure 'the dignity of the individual and the unity of the nation'. The Constitution contains wonderful ideas, suffused with human values and expressing the will of the nation to implement them; but in the Constitution itself, these are only aspirations and promises; their translation into social realities depends upon the free citizens of our democracy, their elected representatives, and the various human management institutions of the country. It is unfortunate that the Constitution failed to stress the fundamental duties of our citizens, while putting due stress on their fundamental rights. A complete philosophy of life will be a happy balance between rights and privileges, on the one hand, and duties and responsibilities, on the other.

The exclusive stress on fundamental rights has resulted in a general clamour by individuals and groups for rights and privileges from the nation; and this clamour has drowned the great humanistic and ethical values of duties and responsibilities. It is time that we correct this imbalance, before the contemporary wrong attitude takes the nation down beyond retrieval.

Even in America, one of her thinkers had suggested that the statue of Liberty in the east coast must be supplemented by a statue of Responsibility in the west coast. And our people must consider today, in the interest of a balanced education of our nation, the value of erecting a statue of Freedom on one side, and a statue of Responsibility on the other side, of our Rajpath in New Delhi. It is time that every segment of our free citizens develops a sense of national responsibility and ask a question to themselves: What do we owe to our nation and how can we discharge that national responsibility? The people have to realize that they have to work hard to build up their nation; they have also to learn that they have to work together with other people; and that means that they have to achieve a certain inner growth to be able to do teamwork. We succeed in so working together when we stress the common goals in front of us more, and our own egos and its profit and pleasure less. These are what constitute the virtues and graces of democratic citizenship, in which individual freedom is wedded to social responsibility.

Freedom of the individual is fundamental to human growth; it is also fundamental to a democratic socio-political order. But that freedom becomes a menace, as much to the individual as to the nation and its demo-cracy, if it fails to inspire itself with a second value, namely, the sense of social responsibility. Along with its wedding to this sense of social responsibility, the free-dom of the individual needs to be enriched with the democratic virtues of self-discipline and a humanly oriented will. This constitutes character, character centred in a socially oriented will. It is this training in citizenship virtues and graces that makes a people, any people, capable of enriching all inter-human relations, including all management techniques, with ethical and humanistic impulses and growth-oriented practical efficiency.

It is obvious that we have not wedded that sense of responsibility and self-discipline to our freedom. We as a people possess the least sense of social responsibility among the peoples of the world; more so, our so-called educated section. We are not willing to respond to the great challenges before our nation. Our common people, on the other hand, have been, and are, hard-working; our deft-fingered artisans create things of beauty and utility by hard work; but they are not able to enjoy the fruits of their honest labour; they are deprived of it by our so-called intelligentsia. Our common people have learned the work ethic; but our educated intelligentsia have not, except when it concerns their own self-interest, and so, they exploit the common people, either remaining lazy themselves or by hard work for their own self-advancement. This has to be changed. Everyone has to learn to do a day's honest labour and then, only then, enjoy the fruit of it in the form of wages and salaries. This is the Bhagvad-Gita philosophy of work, which is followed more by the people ouside India, than by people within India. No nation can become great, or achieve prosperity, without its people developing a sense of self-discipline, social responsibility, and capacity and willingness to do hard, efficient, co-operative work.

III

Some of the profoundest ideas relating to the philo-sophy of work are to be found in our Bhagvad-Gita. It is unique in its stress on work-ethics. Among the great religious books of the past, this is the only book whose central theme is work, man at work, and man achieving from work a double benefit, namely, social welfare outside, and spiritual growth within. All other religious books, Indian or foreign, deal with man at worship, at prayer, at meditation, at ritual. But the Gita deals primarily with man at work – it may be any field of work or any profession – and presents worship, prayer, meditation and ritual as means for man's spiritual growth, development and realization, on the one hand, and for increasing his work-efficiency, leading to social welfare, on the other. This is yoga, the comprehensive philosophy of life and action, capable of ensuring individual and collective human welfare. That philosophy is available to our people today to help us to achieve, through effective administrative and management techniques and better inter-human relationships, our national objectives of total human development and fulfilment for all our people, for the first time in our long history. This possibility is revealed by the testament of the last verse of the Gita itself, which is of great significance today to us. It has remained a mere testament so long; it is the privilege of the people of India, in this modern period, to fully implement that testament:

> Yatra yogeśvaraḥ kṛṣṇo
> yatra pārtho dhanur-dharaḥ;
> Tatra śrī-vijayo bhūtiḥ,
> dhruva nītir-matir-mama...

'Wherever there is Krishna, the master of Yoga, and Arjuna, the wielder of the bow, there (in that society) shall be found wealth, victory, general welfare, and unwavering justice and ethical sense – this is my conviction.'

The verse refers to the confluence, in each person, of two energies needed to achieve total human welfare: the first is the energy of Yoga, the energy of vision, of calm spirituality, represented by Sri Krishna, who, in the Mahabharata war did not take part in the actual fighting, but only gave sagely guidance to Arjuna; and the second is the energy of intense and efficient action, represented by Arjuna, the hero of action. This represents the combination of contemplation and action, vision and implementation, in every citizen, which the Gita and the Chinese philosophy of Taoism call the state of being sagely within and kingly without. Herbert Spencer, in his *Study of Sociology*[3], calls it as 'uniting philanthropic energy with philosophic calm'. This is true education. When this is achieved by people, all management and administration will achieve the highest level of efficiency.

The first fruit of that confluence, says the verse, is *Śrī*, economic prosperity, which our Constitution has set before us as the basic national objective – banishing the demon of dismal mass poverty. This needs not only knowledge and hard work, but also the capacity for dedication and teamwork, which is the gift of character-energy. The smile of *Śrī* or *Lakṣmī*, i.e. wealth, must illumine every hamlet and home in our country. That can come only after first bringing into every hamlet and home the smile of *Sarasvatī*, the goddess of knowledge; and this knowledge, to be true knowledge, always must be accompanied by character. And such knowledge, when applied to work, produces, *Śrī* or *Lakṣmī*. The relationship of *Sarasvatī* to *Lakṣmī* is similar to the relationship of pure science to applied science; and both are needed to achieve total human welfare.

The second fruit of that confluence is *vijaya*, victory, which means, success accompanying every project, every endeavour. The failures or the low-level performances of many of our national projects and undertakings can be traced to the absence, in many of our people, of that confluence wherever success has been registered, we can detect the presence of that blessed confluence.

The third fruit of that confluence is *bhūtiḥ*, general welfare. *Śrī* and *bhūtiḥ* together constitute welfare, which is the socio-economic and cultural objective our Constitution has placed before the nation; and to enable us to achieve that high objective, we need a fourth value.

And the verse refers to that fourth value as *dhruva nītiḥ*, constant justice and ethical sense. No political system, no society, can be healthy without unwavering justice and ethical sense. This is the value called *dharma*, which holds the scale even between individuals and individuals, between groups and groups; by favouring one individual or group and discriminating against another individual or group, we increase injustice in society, increase social discontent, and pave the way for eventual social chaos. Hence the citizens, as much as the administration, must be imbued with justice and ethical sense. This value, referred to above as *dharma*, is presented by Indian Philosophy as the principle that integrates man with man in society. It is basically a by-product of the spiritual growth of the individual citizen, which is expressed as moral law, and which is reinforced by the state laws and regulations. A respect for law and the constant effort to uphold it, on the part of the citizen and of the holders of power in the state, are what make for human integration and the strength and stability of a state, more especially of a democratic state like ours. It is the awakened moral sense in the citizen that expresses itself as human values and that makes the laws and regulations of the state effective. If the moral sense is absent, the laws become ineffective, as the citizens twist the laws to suit their own advantage. This increases injustice in society and weakens the political and social fabric. If the moral sense is not present, social contracts become ineffective; for it is the moral sense that motivates one to stick to a contract; without it, he or she can, and will, flout it.

Thus the basis of our full national development is the vision of 'the Dignity of the Individual and the Unity of the Nation', as enshrined in our Constitution, getting effectively implemented by the combined efforts of self-disciplined citizens and dedicated and efficient executives and employees of the Union and State and all public welfare enterprises. We classify all nations today as developed, underdeveloped, and backward. Our country belongs to the second category. How did the developed nations of today acquire the developed status? They were, some centuries ago, less developed than we are today. In the 15th and 16th centuries, there was much poverty and squalor in Europe. Then came the spread of education among the masses, hard work, co-operative work, and human concern. They became developed, modern science and technology accelerating the process. Thus education on national scale, self-discipline, hard and co-operative work, and the human-istic impulse – these are the four means by which under-developed India will become a fully developed nation, with enormous disciplined energies released from her vast population. We thus free ourselves from our feudal past and become a modern progressive democratic nation, constituting one-seventh of humanity.

IV

What makes a static system of administration and management dynamic is the human orientation. There the heart is touched, not the mere intellect. It is when heart responds to heart that a static bureaucracy and management become transformed into dynamic developmental administration and management. There is an appropriate strategy in every thing. Our people and even our foreign collaborators in industry often complain that nothing moves in our bureaucracy; how many well-conceived developmental plans and programmes in our country are getting stifled by our wooden bureaucracy! All this will change when all our public service activities become infused with an enlightened citizenship-awareness and the humanistic motive; every file in front will then evoke in the employee, sitting on the office chair, the human response to the human urges and needs of people, living far and near, which the file represents.

When human urges and aspirations for a better life invade the hearts of millions of people, whose life had been dismal and stagnant for centuries, but who, becoming aroused by the economic and social possibilities of the modern revolutionary age, resolve to take advantage of them and set to work for their betterment, they keenly feel the need for finance and capital; and the bank goes to their help with finance and thus sets in motion the developmental process. Earlier, there was the ubiquitous money lender; in spite of his high interest rates, which have ruined many families, his role was also social service, but not with the service, but a high profit motive, and relevant to a static socio-economic order only; it was not meant to produce new wealth, not meant for socio-economic development, but merely to shuffle poverty and wealth among the population. In this context appeared the institution of modern banking. In its earlier stages, it was established by a few people, who were mostly money-lenders turned businessmen or industrialists, with a view to finding finances for their own or their friends' business or industrial ventures. The scope of such banking was very restricted and was not capable of playing a national role. That restricted role of banking became changed in the wake of political freedom and the nation-wide initiation of socio-economic development activities. This led to nationalization and the quick spread of banking institutions, first in the urban, then in the rural areas; this process is getting accelerated year by year until the nation reaches the national target of one bank for a specified number of the population.

As with everything else in India, this spreading wide of the tree of banking into every nook and corner of the nation, as it is now, and as it will be later when the national target is achieved, is only a quantitative expansion; such quantitative expansion calls for a *pari passu* qualitative enrichment. Our quantitative expansion has been colossal, since independence, with respect to our Union and State Bureaucracies, banking, State Trading Corporation, L.I.C., and other service institutions, as also in our population. But what all our proliferating institutions stand in urgent need of today is a qualitative enrichment. That calls for the infusion of human values in their operation; and these human values do not proceed from buildings and equipments, rules and regulations, organizations and systems; they unfold from the depth of the human personality; they manifest under the guidance of an adequate philosophy of life, but get stifled and blunted under the guidance of a wrong philosophy of life and work. Values are not mechanical, says the agnostic thinker Bertrand Russell:

> The Machine is the modern form of Satan, and its worship is the modern diabolism.... Whatever else may be mechanical, values are not, and this is something which no political philosopher must forget.[4]

Indian wisdom, as expressed in Vedanta, holds that a philosophy of values is a part of, and derives from a philosophy of man in all his heights and depths; it holds that man creates values from within himself in the context of his interactions with nature and society without. Out of the two, he only manipulates nature, but he both manipulates, and enters, and is manipulated and entered into by, other human beings in society. It is while doing so that he becomes the focus of values and experiences fulfilment. Thus values are specifically the products of evolution at the human stage, and are spiritual in nature, in the sense that they arise from the inner spiritual nature of man.

V

It is instructive to study human values in the light of comprehensive Hindu concept of the four *puruṣārthas*, i.e. values sought after by *puruṣa* or man. These are: *dharma, artha, kāma* and *mokṣa*. In its scale of values, Vedanta finds an honoured place for all desires and urges of man, from the material and sensory to the moral, ethical, and super-sensory or transcendental. The Sanskrit word and concept, *kāma*, desire, constitutes the entire range of human cravings and satisfactions at the sensory level; it is the first of the *puruṣārtha*s. The second *puruṣārtha* is *artha*, wealth, which is the instrument for the satisfaction of *kāma*. The third *puruṣārtha* is known as *dharma*, which means ethical sense, and which helps to discipline and regulate the pursuit of the first and the second, so that all persons in a society get the opportunity to satisfy their urge for them. Human values in management and administration proceed from this third *puruṣārtha* of *dharma*; though third in order from the point of view of human experience, it is put first in all enumerations, due to its primacy and importance. This *dharma* is essentially what manifests spontaneously as a by-product of man's inner growth, of man's spiritual growth, from the freedom of individuality to the freedom and social responsibility of personality. The first is *vyāktitva*, the second is *vikāśita vyāktitva*. These terms, person and personality, are defined by the British biologist and humanist, late Sir Julian Huxley thus ('Introduction' to *The Phenomenon of Man* by Teilhard de Chardin):

> Persons are individuals who transcend their organic individuality in conscious (social) participation.

This growth from individuality to personality is a spiritual growth which transforms mere *gṛhastha* or householder, who is genetically limited in his or her sympathies and interests, into a citizen whose sympathies and interests become nationwide, and also international, cutting across all genetic and other limitations. This is *vyāktitva*, individuality, but *vikāśita*, i.e. expanded, beyond physical or genetic limitations. It is this second step in spiritual growth – the first step being individuality itself, an awareness of one's individual identity, dignity, and worth – that makes for enlightened citizenship in a democracy.

Human values manifest spontaneously in man as person, but only artificially and with effort in man as mere individual. When man as a person, as an enlightened citizen, becomes an employee of public service, institutions like banks or government secretariat offices, human values become manifest, and qualitatively enrich the work of those institutions. Such a person will not think of himself or herself as a mere employee, but as a free citizen of India called by the nation to perform a particular service to the people. This is what transforms work into a mission, into a national commitment; and this is also what enhances the dignity of the worker, from being a mere employee, or paid servant, into an instrument of human purposes. A clerk's work, done with a clerk's mind, makes that clerk and his work small; but the same work, done with a citizen's mind and attitude, elevates both the work and the worker. This is the philosophy of work taught in the Bhagavad-Gita. This is echoed in an oft-quoted sentence of the British thinker, late Bernard Shaw: 'This is the true joy in life – to be used for a purpose which you consider mighty; to be a force of nature, and not a clod of ailments and grievances, ever complaining that the world does not devote itself to making you happy'.

It is this attitudinal transformation, this enlightened citizenship attitude, that must invade the hearts and minds of all our (at present *ad hoc* and nominal) citizens in general, and also of all the millions of employees of all our secretariats, banks, and other public service institutions, in particular. This is the importance of that third *puruṣārtha* or value referred to earlier, namely, *dharma*, which, in this context, does not mean any dogma or creed or theological belief or religious ritual, but only the growth of man from a self-centred individual, seeking only his or her own freedom and self-interest, to a free and socially responsible person, seeking one's freedom and self-interest in the context of the freedom and self-interest of all others in society.

In this, we see the genetically limited *gṛhastha* or house-holder growing, becoming spiritually evolved, into the citizen. This growth is much needed by all in India, for, since several centuries, we have degenerated into being good *gṛhastha*s but bad citizens. The *gṛhastha* as citizen, endowed with awareness by his or her social responsibility and discharging it well, is highly praised in the Hindu tradition. In the glowing words of the Manusmriti (3. 77-78):

Yathā vāyum samāśritya sarve jivanti jāntavaḥ;
Tathā gṛhasthamāśritya vartante sarva-āśramaḥ

'Just as all creatures live depending on air, so do all

*āśrama*s, (namely, *brahmacari* or student, *vānaprastha* or forest-dweller after retirement, and *yati* or all-renouncing monk or nun) exist depending on the *gṛhastha* or citizen-householder'.

> *Yasmāt trayo'pyaśramino*
> *jñānenannena cānvaham;*
> *Gṛhasthenaiva dhāryante,*
> *tasmāt jyeṣṭhaśrāmi gṛhī.*

'Because of the fact that the three other *āśramas* are always supported and nourished with knowledge and food by the *gṛhastha* alone, therefore the *gṛhastha* is the most excellent *āśrama*'.

Vedanta philosophy, therefore, treats these three, namely, *dharma, artha,* and *kāma* as the *trivarga*, the triple set, always going together ensure the happiness and welfare of all. Their presence together in any society makes for material progress, cultural development, and general welfare of its diverse population.

Vedanta designated the fourth and last *puruṣārtha* by the word *mokṣa*, which means full spiritual freedom; it is a super-sensory and trans-social dimension of experience, but not super-natural. Unlike as in Christianity and all other Semitic religions, which uphold the super-natural and thus come into conflict with physical science, there is no concept of the super-natural in Vedanta, since its concept of nature, or *prakṛti*, is wide enough to embrace the two dimensions of one and the same reality, namely, the dimensions of the physical and the secular – *aparā prakṛti*, and the super-physical and the spiritual – *parā prakṛti*. It is the unique state of joyous aloneness (in contrast to painful loneliness), in which man ceases to be gregarious. 'In the last stages of life's journey, man walks in single file', says Dr. S. Radhakrishnan. As in Everest climbing, we start as a crowd at the base camp, the number decreases steadily as the climbing progresses, and, at the very summit, we proceed in single file; meditation, in daily life, represents this experience of aloneness, of non-gregariousness.

Though thus trans-social, the *mokṣa* value has tremendous invisible impact on society, by strengthening the power of *dharma* to achieve human integration in society, be it through citizenship confined to a nation or that same citizenship reaching out to the international and human dimensions. For *dharma* is only that *mokṣa* ideal and experience expressed in and through the social context. The Vedanta has expounded this concept of the four *puruṣārthas* keeping in view humanity as a whole, and not a segment of it, like nation, caste, or creed. *Artha* and *kāma*, under the guidance of *dharma*, are wholesome; but they become harmful without that guidance. Sri Krishna praises such *kāma* in the Gita (7. 11):

> *Dharmāviruddho bhūteṣu*
> *Kāmo'smi bharatarṣabha –*

'I am that *kāma* in all beings that is unopposed to *dharma*'.

This dissatisfaction with, and going beyond, the *kāma* and *artha* to *dharma* and *mokṣa* values is uniquely a human possibility; without that further step, human life stagnates, and the pursuit of *kāma* and *artha* becomes abnormal and unhealthy as much for the individual concerned as for the society. It is *dharma* and *mokṣa* pursuits that lift human life above the animal life: *dharmena hīnaḥ, paśubhiḥ samānaḥ* – 'bereft of *dharma*, man is just an animal', says an oft-quoted verse of the Hindu tradition. In his *Gita Rahasya* (p. 156), Lokmanya Tilak quotes the following words of the materialistic English philosopher of the last century, John Stuart Mill, which will be interesting in this context (Utilitarianism, p. 14):

> It is better to be a human being dissatisfied than a pig satisfied; better to be a Socrates dissatisfied than a fool satisfied. And if the fool, or the pig, is of a different opinion, it is because they only know their own side of the question.

The Hindu spiritual tradition teaches us (Manusmriti, 4.176):

> *Parityājet artha-kāmau*
> *yau syatam dharma-varjitau;*
> *Dharmam capyasukhodarkam*
> *loka-vikrustameva ca.*

'Give up those *artha*s and *kāma*s (wealth and sensory cravings) which are opposed to *dharma*; and (give up) even that *dharma* which results in one's own unhappiness (like donating all wealth without thought for the care of one's children) and in the suffering of the people.'

Thus earning wealth by right means and honest labour is *dharmic*, but greed, and its impulsion to dishonesty and unscrupulousness, is opposed to *dharma*; it is opposed to *dharma* means, it is opposed to general social welfare and one's own inner spiritual growth, it is *dharma* that equalizes a strong man and a weak man in society; if the restraint of *dharma* is not there, the strong will have all the *kāma* and *artha*, and the weak will be deprived of even elementary human satisfactions; and that was what obtained in our feudal social order, where the haves monopolized all the good things of life and the have-nots were left to live a near-animal life. This is what we have to change fully in our democracy, by infusing moral, ethical, and human values into our society.

VI

In this context, I wish to point out that our people have to learn afresh the true meaning and significance of the two important Hindu concepts of *Sarasvatī* and *Lakṣmī*. *Sarasvatī* stands for knowledge – not the dead knowledge which is the product of investigation into the truth of nature and of man. *Lakṣmī*, similarly, means not just wealth, but wealth invested in productive enterprises; it means wealth and welfare resulting from the application of knowledge through efficient and co-operative work; *Sarasvati*, accordingly represents, in modern knowledge and language, pure science, and *Lakṣmī* represents applied science. Thus *Lakṣmī* flows from *Sarasvatī*; these two are not jealous sisters, by which where one is, the other will not be, as our perverted belief in our decadent period of history told us. The same decadent period also told us that the worship of these beautiful goddesses consists mainly in doing rituals before their images or pictures, and not in the tapas of knowledge-seeking and in the tapas of hard work in the fields, factories, workshops, and offices.

This is the lesson that our nation has to learn today in a big way, so that we may succeed in banishing the demons of ignorance and poverty from our land, which was known in ancient world history as the land of wisdom and wealth. Modern Western history teaches us this truth, that these two goddesses are friendly sisters and that first comes the worship of *Sarasvatī* through scientific research and the acquisition, assimilation, and distribution of knowledge, and that this is followed by the worship of *Lakṣmī*, through the application of knowledge in all fields of human development and welfare. The integrated play of the energies of *Sarasvatī* and *Lakṣmī* in a society is what the last verse of the Gita expounds, as I had explained it earlier.

Our country needs to manifest greater and greater energy, in the true form of worship of *Sarasvatī*, by the steady spread of education and enlightenment among all our people. Imagine the mental energy resources that will become available to our nation, if all our immense population is educated at least up to the eighth standard; it will be still better if every one completes at least the higher secondary level. With such widespread education, there will ensure unprecedented productive and other economic activities, which will result in an unprecedented expansion of employment opportunities and banking services as well. All revolution in productive enterprises, which represents the play of *Lakṣmī*, depends upon a prior revolution in education and research, which is the play of *Sarasvatī*.

SWAMI RANGANATHANANDA

References:

1. *Letters of Swamy Vivekananda*, 4th ed., p. 175.
2. *Ibid.*, p. 111.
3. *Ibid.*, p. 404.
4. Bernard Russell: *Impact of Science on Sociology*. p. 77.

THE SPIRITUO-TECHNICAL APPROACH
TO MANAGEMENT

Management: A 'Lever' for higher life

Be it individual, family or farm; be it State, business or industry; be it art, profession or administration, one aspires to attain a high degree of performance and pursuit, this calls for productivity with peace and growth with harmony. And these are encompassed by good management. If any single factor is the key for unlocking the force of growth with prosperity, that factor is MANAGEMENT. If achieved, production is indicative of material growth, and productivity a dynamic condition facilitating acceleration of goods and services, but management can serve as a 'lever' for higher life based on values, ethics and consciousness. Production is increased by material incentives, says one School of Thought; it is increased rather by the impulsion of political and social idealism, says another School; but a third School maintains that it is the injection of sound management based on consciousness – from within-to-without management – that stimulates real prosperity.

II

Management has acquired steadily increasing importance as we proceeded to modern industrialised society. Not only has modern industry grown to be such a bewilderingly octopus-organisation, it has also to be sustained by equally complex collateral agencies of all kinds – say for marketing the products, siphoning finance, maintaining public relations, recruiting labour-force, training specialist-technicians and for conducting research towards newer and still newer products and processes of production or more and more attractive baits for the avid consumerist society.

III

But management can have meaning only in relation to specified ends, and the means available or mobilisable to achieve these ends. Given the ends or goals, management must consist in assembling the means, organising them to a condition of integral prosperity and effecting further improvements. These ideas are by no means so novel as they may be made to sound. Our hoary word 'Yoga' could mean addition, the injection or introduction of ideas or disciplines leading to a charging of power, a heightening of productivity and a quickening or enlargement of results. Yoga could lead to Kshema, the efflorescence of welfare. If work is worship, purposeful work could lead verily to Realisation. There can be no planning, no productivity, no management, no Loka Kshema, no Sarvodaya or sunrise of universal well-being without the readiness of the people to work with a sense of common aims, a perceived sense of common direction and a converging feeling of total dedication and higher consciousness.

Vain indeed is all overweening pride in the conquest even of the entire universe if one has not conquered one's own passions.

Without the mastery of one's own ego, the containment of the turbulent enemy within, of what avail is the manipulation of mere techniques? Self and self-management was the talk of Arnold Bennett's popular guides. The physician who can heal himself, the man who can master himself and manage efficiently his own affairs, starts under right auspices when he sets out on the career of others. Management Development cannot take place without Self-Development.

IV

Modern Management: Materialist, Professional, Soul-less

But management, as it obtains today, is a technique imported from the West. It is not germane to Indian soil. It is not based on Indian heritage. We have already entered into the age of computers and robots when, perhaps, human mind and hands are sought to be eliminated. Excessive technological growth has created an environment in which life has become physically and mentally unhealthy. They concentrate on 'production targets' and 'profit and loss accounts', thus losing leverage to engineer a 'turn-around' and believe that the 'balance sheet' of human talent is of secondary importance in the organisation.

Management, which was once a personal and direct action has now grown into an indirect feat and phenomenon. This change in the management system has brought in a lure for materialism and the race for production and distribution has brought forth a lust for profit all-round. Ends rule supreme, means are discounted. Management has been reduced to be a handmaid of profiteering. The maximising of profits becomes the ultimate goal, to the exclusion of all other considerations. 'This technology is fragmented rather than holistic, bent on manipulation and control rather than co-operation, self-assertive rather than integrative, and suitable for centralised management rather than regional application by individuals and small groups. As a result, the technology has become profoundly anti-ecological, anti-social, unhealthy, and inhuman.'[1] And this pattern of management naturally rests upon giant-like industries, massive and round-the-clock production and productivity of the worker. 'Productivity is usually defined as the output per employee per working hour. To increase this quantity, manufacturers tend to automate and mechanize the production process as much as possible. However, in doing so they increase the number of unemployed workers and lower their productivity to zero by adding them to the welfare rolls.'[2]

V

The core of modern management thought is the worker (MAN?) – an efficient workman, a skilful functionary and a productive member of the work-force. They are paid more so that they may work more and better; they are rewarded and reimbursed so that they remain locked-up with management as a lever of contributing profits. This has brought into fore management and workers as separate entitites – their approach is different, their interests are diverse and their claims are conflicting. There has remained no more common approach and understanding between members of a management hierarchy.

To the modern management, the worker is all. MAN stands nowhere. The moment he ceases to be serviceable he stands discarded, like a hired commodity, and is promptly replaced. The work-force, too, resorts to underhand pressures just to extract as much as possible to dupe the management. Conflicts are common, violence is rampant, absenteeism is the rule and strikes and breakdowns are daily occurrences.

VI

This materialistic management has done more harm than good. The capitalist has grown richer, man has been reduced to a hired wage-earner and the consumer has been placed at the mercy of the materialist-manager. There is no sense of belonging, no harmony, no co-operative organisation, no fellow-feelings and the least common approach and perspective.

One obvious result of this pernicious form of modern management has been disregard of human approach, loss of human values and erosion of human touch. The crisis of confidence prevails in all camps. The society has suffered and deteriorated, the worker has remained demoralised, the consumer has been by-passed and man has suffered loss of dignity and his due.

The manager, too, is not a net gainer. He has earned

millions but only at the cost of his peace and sound
sleep. He suffers from insomnia, gastric complaints,
high blood-pressure, heart-ailments and mental discomforts. He fattens his coffers but suffers from mental
unrest. Labour troubles, production losses, erosion of
markets, tax measures and reduction of profits haunt his
mind yielding only sleeplessness and resort to sleeping
pills. Wealth is gained but peace is lost. No wonder,
therefore, that the materialist management of the
Western style has remained to be only a 'soul-less
management'.

VII

In a cynical way, of course, one may deploy the four
classic means of sama-dama-danda-bheda. There is the
tactful and conciliatory way littered with sweet speech;
there is the way of bribing, carrot-waving, sugar-plum
offering; there is devious divide-and-rule tactics; and
there is the way of attack, revenge, deprivation, brandishing the big stick, giving no quarter. People are
ordinarily moved by flattery, greed, suspicion and fear,
and the manager is free to exploit one or more or all of
these only too common emotions and passions and
inducements. But this may not take him far, or not for a
long time. Without hard-won knowledge, a gift of vision
or feeling for perspective, a total sense of responsibility
and an approach of consciousness, one must sooner or
later, mess up management and fail as a manager.

There can be, one might say, two attitudes in
general to life and life's work. There is the attitude

of separate acquisition and possession or competition, anxiety and strain. There is another one of relative freedom, of detachment, of relaxation and of self-consecration.[3]

The latter attitude is born of a spiritual world-view, as distinct from the materialist view-point. If one must think of the enemy, he is everywhere and there can be no escape from him. Then, why not think of the enemy as the friend, why not transcend the duality of enemy and friend?

VIII

Fresh Thinking Necessary:
Man: Primary Input
Management: Developmental Discipline

It becomes imperative, therefore, that fresh thinking is done so as to underline the development of man in contrast to mere development of a wage-earner. Akito Morita, the creator of SONY, who treats his employees as members of his family declares:

> Machines and computers do not make business a success; it is the people. Similarly, no theory or plan will make business a success that can only be done with people.

Technology makes things possible but it is the people who make it happen. Man is thus the primary input to management process. Man is the first syllable in MA-Nagement. Any worker, whatever category he belongs to, is first a MAN and then a worker. His needs and demands, as a human being, are no less important, rather more important than his claims as a wage-earner. His needs as a man are not merely his physical needs of food and shelter or even his needs and aspirations as a member of a group or a family. A man is not merely a mass of flesh, blood and bones. He is a mental creature in a physical frame. A worker as a man is a pack of feelings, emotions, sentiments, likes and dislikes, priorities and preferences. He has his physique, his vitals, mind, heart, spirit and soul. He is an awakened entity with consciousness. His conscience speaks; his soul guides. He has to be contented for his physical needs, satiated for his mental demands but satisfied for his needs and demands of the soul.

> In this investiture of fleshy life,
> A soul that is a spark of God survives.
> And sometimes it breaks through the sordid screen
> And kindles a fire that makes us half-divine.[4]

Man is an integrated creature of the Divine Craftsman. His man is more important than our worker. There is nothing like a hierarchy of needs, as claimed by Western Thought. All needs go together and simultaneously all needs are equally and parallelly important and pressing. The workers' vision has shifted from merely meeting their physiological needs to the 'quality of life', 'human enrichment' and 'self-actualisation'.

Incentives are important for motivating men towards more and better work. But no human motivation can be generated and sustained for long by merely paying wages and bonuses. Managers must ponder over such steps as justice and fairness in thought and action, sincerity of purpose and words, awakening of consciousness, feelings of patriotism and nationalism, spontaneity of actions, aesthetic values, creation and satisfaction of higher aspirations, promotion of goodwill and oneness, behavioural decencies, satisfaction of religious and moral aspirations, human touch, sense of spirituality through instructional and behavioural programmes and organisational adjustments.

In the changed social order, management ceases to be a career discipline; it must be taken as a developmental process. Man has to be dressed up and developed in an integrated form and size. The management approach has to be focussed upon development of man and society and not merely to train and retrain a worker. The worker has to be made soul-conscious – that he is being guided by his inner being to serve the Divine through his work and behaviour. Human development in an organisation should be the aim of all management programmes. The management should do all that helps the workers to develop their physique, broaden their outlook, energise their mental faculties, grow their consciousness and enrich their soul.

Man, as such, is an imperfect being – his mind is only an instrument of thought and action and not a source of knowledge.

> A thinking puppet is the mind of life,
> Its choice is the work of elemental strengths,
> That know not their own birth and end and cause
> And glimpse not the immense intent they have.[5]

Knowledge emerges from the inner being. Hence, the inner being of the man has to be suitably developed in order to make him creative and responsive. Sincerity should be his principal tool of action. Management can do so not by mere words but more by actions. Management should be action-oriented − they should do themselves what they want to be done by others. The substance is: a good man with a noble heart and soul shall make a good and responsible worker, although the opposite may not be true. On this aspect of man and management let us read what Sri Aurobindo has said:

> For man intellectually developed, mighty in scientific knowledge and mastery of gross and subtle nature, using the elements as his servants and the world as his footstool, but, undeveloped in heart and spirit, becomes only an inferior kind of *Asura* using the powers of a demigod to satisfy the nature of an animal.[6]

Explicit reference to human attitudes, values and life-styles in future management thought will make this new science profoundly humanistic. It will deal with human aspirations and potentialities and will integrate them into the underlying matrix of the global approach. Such an approach will transcend by far anything attempted hitherto in the field of management system. In its ultimate nature it will be scientific and spiritual at the same time.

IX

Yoga in Management:
Yoga: Quest for Divine
Management: Search for Loka Kshema

While suggesting a consciousness approach to management, let us be frank to admit that the process of
management, as developed in the West and adopted in
India, does not make a subject of discredit now to be
discarded as wholly unsuitable by any measure. The
system has remained in vogue for decades in the past
and had also delivered goods in the context of the then
prevailing conditions when man had not awakened to
his SELF and mind was the only controlling factor in all
human activities. The actions of the management had
been guided by mind which was considered, although
ignorantly and erroneously, to be the summit of human
evolution.

We may listen to Sri Aurobindo on this point:

> The spirit that manifests itself in man dominates
> secretly the phases of his development, is greater
> and profounder than his intellect and drives to-
> wards a perfection that cannot be shut in by the
> arbitrary constructions of human reason.[6a]

And likewise Einstein has cautioned us:

> Certainly we should take care not to make the
> intellect our God; it has of course powerful
> muscles, but no personality. It cannot lead, it can
> only serve; and it is not fastidious about its choice

of leader.... The intellect has a sharp eye for
methods and tools, but is blind to ends and values.[6b]

But there is something beyond mind (Dharma, Consciousness) which has been discovered now to regulate
all human endeavours.

There is a being beyond the being of mind,
An Immeasurable cast into many forms,
A miracle of the multitudinous one,
There is a consciousness mind cannot touch.
Its speech cannot utter nor its thought reveal.[7]

Beyond mind is the inner being — Truth Consciousness (Divine Adesh) which regulates all human
activities. In the changed context of things, therefore,
management has to shift its reliance from mind to
Consciousness so that management may become an
instrument of human development and global welfare;
so that the narrow parameters of managing personnel
be broadened to bring within their fold the human
good, social virtues and universal welfare.

Spirit, not mind, should be the guide; Sarvodaya, not
selfishness, should be the goal and harmony, not conflict, should be the process. We have crossed over the
age of mind and now we have to enter upon the Age of
Spirit — a realm of consciousness.

X

One may well ask here the role and relevance of Yoga
in management. Well, Yoga begins when man awakens

to an existence beyond mind, when he senses inward and seeks to discover the Divine in himself.

> Yoga is not a thing of ideas but of inner spiritual experience... Yoga means a change of consciousness; a mere mental activity will not bring a change of consciousness, it can only bring a change of mind. And if your mind is sufficiently mobile, it will go on changing from one thing to another till the end without arriving at any sure way or any spiritual harbour.... There are only three ways by which it can make itself a channel or instrument of Truth. Either it must fall silent in the Self and give room for a wider and greater consciousness; or it must make itself passive to an inner Light and allow that Light to use it as a means of expression; or else, it must itself change from the questioning intellectual superficial mind it now is to an intuitive intelligence, a mind of vision fit for the direct perception of the Divine Truth.
>
> (SRI AUROBINDO, *Letters on Yoga*, 1971, p. 161.)

By this quest, he grows in consciousness and lives in a higher plane of existence with a more illumined knowledge, purer, vaster love and more purposeful will in action. Initially, to contact the Divine, man resorts to prayer and, at its highest, prayer becomes an aspiration from the soul for any worldly end. At this point Yoga works. Later, it leads to consecration which means doing an act as an offering to the Divine. Then the Divine in life responds to the inner effort and the outer life becomes an expression of the inner consecration.

This way, a manager can also become a Yogi who starts with an inner prayer for the success of his organisation, consecrates his business as a surrender to the Divine and aspires for Divine Grace for the growth and development of his business towards the progress of his organisation, welfare of his workers, customers and consumers. He consecrates his work to the Divine, relies on his inner being and invokes the progress and welfare of society. While he acts in the world he remains in Divine Consciousness through prayer, consecration and aspiration for progress and welfare of all concerned because 'imperfect is the joy not shared by all'.

> A prayer, a master act, a king idea,
> Can link man's strength to a transcendent Force
> Then miracle is made the common rule,
> One mighty deed can change the course of things;
> A lonely thought becomes omnipotent.[8]

Sri Aurobindo, in his scheme of "Transformation to Supermind" declares that 'All Life is Yoga'. The business manager is not excluded from it. No business is black and no management is bad – all depends upon the attitude, the spirit, the consciousness in which management is done, the principles on which it is built and the purpose it is turned to. Even War can be spiritual, provided it aims at establishing the reign of God. Lord Krishna had exhorted Arjuna to carry on war of the most terrible kind. Nobody thinks that Krishna was an unspiritual man and his advice to Arjuna was unspiritual in principle. A manager by doing in the right way and in the right spirit the work dictated to him by his fundamental nature, temperament and capacity and according to his or its dharma can become spiritual and move to the Divine. All that is necessary is that management must act without self-desire, without any egoistic attitude or motive but as an offering or sacrifice to the Divine. The rest comes from the Divine Grace!

XI

**The Consciousness Approach:
Aspiration, Consecration, Introspection
Within-to-Without Management**

About the Consciousness Approach, let us understand that there is a direct correspondence between man's inner life of thought, feelings and impulses – his inner attitude – to the events in his external life. All that is external is the reflex of his inner condition. When a conscious effort is made to change oneself within, life responds to that change.

> Our outward happenings have their seeds within.
> The Laws of the Unknown create the known.[9]

> On inner values hangs the Outer plan.[10]

Hence, all that is essential is to develop one's inner being – develop one's own attitude, one's awareness, one's consciousness. Rightly said, if one changes one's consciousness the whole world itself changes for you. It is like a pair of green glasses mounted on your vision to see green all round. This depends upon your aspiration and attitude. Consciousness is the 'inner aspect' of life.

> But all is screened, subliminal, mystical.
> It needs the intuitive heart, the inward turn,
> It needs the power of a spiritual gaze.[11]

In management, this relates to the manager's inner attitude towards his organisation, men, material, money, methods and markets. Similarly, in an organisation, this will relate to everyone's attitude towards work and men.

Consciousness is not like skills or technology which may be borrowed or imported ready-made. Nor can consciousness be imparted or transferred, although a business manager can create an environment by his actions and behaviour to provide for an impulse to factors of production – animate and inanimate – to develop their consciousness. Consciousness is an urge which is acquired through faith, dedication, introspection and aspiration for a divine mode of life and living.

> Consciousness is made up of two elements, awareness of self and things and forces and conscious-power. Awareness is the first thing necessary, you have to be aware of things in the right consciousness, in the right way, seeing them in their truth; but awareness by itself is not enough. There must be a Will and a Force that make the consciousness effective. Somebody may have the full consciousness of what has to be changed, what has to go and what has to come in its place, but may be helpless to make the change. Another may have the will-force, but for want of a right awareness

may be unable to apply it in the right way at the right place. The advantage of being in the true consciousness is that you have the right awareness and its will being in harmony with the Mother's will, you can call in the Mother's Force to make the change.... It is only in the supermind that Awareness, Will, Force are always one movement and automatically effective.

(SRI AUROBINDO, *Letters on Yoga*, 1971, p. 238)

Consciousness is something personal, something inner, which knows not price and exchange. 'This is the inner war without escape.'[12]

Based on Consciousness, management has to be developed from "Within-to-Without".

XII

The question arises: How can Consciousness Approach to management be implemented and practised?

Well, the quality of management depends primarily upon the quality and approach of the Top Manager. One expects first and foremost from the man at the top a character, integrity and intellectual honesty, selflessness and objectivity that makes the men trust him and, in difficulty, look up to him. All these are the qualities of heart and the inner being. In Consciousness Approach, too, a beginning will have to be made from those who are at the helm of affairs. First, the Top Executive will have to form a positive attitude to develop his consciousness – he has to be a Yogi, in other words, descending to the depths of his inner being with intense aspiration to invoke Divine Grace towards progress and welfare of his business. It is a battle to control the mind – the self within. In course of time, this will percolate to the lower layers of the organisation. To begin with, he may adopt some steps like these:

1. Aspiration

Forming Basic Attitude: Before embarking upon details let the business manager define his own attitude towards his business: whether his organisation would aim at only amassing wealth, or establishing a business empire, or fleecing the consumer, or be a medium of social progress, or make an instrument to serve the Divine. He has to take the decision with intense aspiration, deepest devotion, perfect objectivity, Yogic approach and strongest conviction towards global welfare. His choice based on his inner being will determine his externalities to achieve the goals. 'Aspiration shows the image of a crown'.[12a]

2. Consecration

Communion with the Divine: Consecration means complete surrender and communion. Let the manager consecrate to the Divine his institution, all the physical paraphernalia, organisational hierarchy, all systems and sub-systems, manpower and everything. Offer these to the service of the Divine and the Divine will take charge of these. Do so with ardent aspiration. By consecration one leaves oneself wholly to the care and charge of the Divine. Then faith develops, conviction comes in and communion grows. All our actions are left to the charge of the Divine care and Grace.

3. Self-Introspection

Search Thyself First: For any fault, for any conflict see within, peep into your inner being and discover if you are on the wrong side in any way, if you carry that fault within yourself and if you are responsible for the breakdown. In difference of opinion take that the other party is right and you may be wrong. From oneself, one has to be one's best judge, and one's own worst critic.

One's own latent capacity for falsehood, slander, ill-will and jealousy, even when unexpressed, leaves one open to overt negativity from others. The best protection is a sincere examination of the roots of such vibration within oneself. Consult your consciousness and apply your objectivity to it. Enter into personal, silent, conscious relationship with every person, system and nourish them by your consciousness. This will solve many of the conflicts, differences and chaos.

Develop the golden attitude: "Others are right, I may be wrong".

4. Meditative Silence:

Decision-making in Peaceful Silence: Faced with a variety of situations, a manager comes across problems pertaining to his day-to-day business-working. Also, he is required to take short and long-term decisions on a variety of problems. To reach solutions, let him retire in perfect peaceful silence, identify with problems, search for alternatives and he will reach the solutions.

In absolute silence sleeps an absolute power.[13]

Silence here does not mean only absence of speech, but a perfect calm in body, mind and heart. Let him retire from life-problems, sit in silence, invoke peace, concentrate on the problems, meditate over the situation and wait for the Divine Grace while reaching the solution.

In the mind's Silence the Transcendent acts
And the hushed heart hears the unuttered word.[14]

In secrecy wraps the seed the Eternal sows
Silence, the mystic birthplace of the soul.[15]

Let there be a 'Room of Silence' attached to his office where he may retire from noisy life to meditate over the problems, in case of need. Let him also provide for such facilities to his employees to retire in silence and seek solutions to their problems. By this method, the manager and his employees gradually come in contact with the Divine and the Divine enters into their outer circumstances.

In moments when the inner lamps are lit,
And the life's cherished guests are left outside,
Our spirit sits alone and speaks to its gulfs,
A wider consciousness opens then its doors.[16]

Hidden in silent depths the word is formed
From hidden silences the act is born.[17]

A work is done in deep silences.[18]

But the suggested meditation in silence should
not be mere ritual and ceremonial. It should not be
only a mental exercise but an inner call to invoke
Divine Grace. Prayer in peace will lend inner
strength and will sustain.

Similarly, the 'Room of Silence' should not be
meant for discussion or any kind of active occupation. Here, one relaxes, keeps oneself open to the
right guidance from within or from above. An
atmosphere is built up where no decision-making
effort is needed; the decision or indication comes
naturally. This is a long-drawn exercise but a beginning can be made to develop one's consciousness.

XIII

In a management process men, materials, machines,
methods and money – all require a certain minimum
care and attention for serving better. The truth is that
the Divine is in all things and all things are Divine. By
giving care and attention in the form of mental interest,
loving care, enthusiasm and physical concern we contact

and respect the Divine in matter. In the Consciousness Approach we may prescribe a programme as under –

1. Study every employee silently to learn his talents and untapped potentials. Attempt to upgrade each employee to his maximum capacity.

Each employee should be conscious of what he contributes and what he receives. Relieve him of any false sense that he gives more than others and/or receives less recognition.

The best way to give attention to men is to take interest in the work they do and give just recognition. No worker will remain indifferent to the sincere concern of the employer for his growth and well-being.

2. Note simple avoidable sources of friction between employees and remove them by silent initiative. Strong criticism delivered in a mean or heartless way is like hitting a man on the head with a hammer. The power of love is infinitely more effective. Kind suggestions, given with love and understanding can accomplish wonders; mere fault-finding accomplishes nothing. One is fit to judge others only after he has perfected his own nature. Till then, judging oneself is the only profitable analysis.

3. Set all machinery and physical paraphernalia in perfect working order. Even the physical things have consciousness. Nurse them with loving care, and they will serve you more and better.

4. Examine every system to see that it is working at maximum efficiency. Each system is a source to be fully utilised.

5. Work to increase cleanliness, orderliness, regularity, punctuality, peace, silence even to a small extent. Cleanliness, orderliness, absence of loud sounds, expression of anger, presence of rhythmic music, murals and fresh flowers – all contribute to creating a positive atmosphere.

6. Remove all areas of distrust, secrecy, hiding etc., where falsehood prevails or which may encourage falsehood.

7. See that all outer events such as mail, calls, obligations are handled as promptly as possible. Ensure work for maximum speed of response.

8. For every outer difficulty or problem, identify the corresponding inner point in the consciousness of management and staff. Consult the Divine and take guidance from Him.

XIV

Conclusion

The basis of Consciousness Approach is thus the link between man's inner being and events in outer life. By changing, therefore, the inner condition, one brings about a responsive change in the external world.

Behind the surface personality in man lies his true inner being. By contacting this deeper centre he frees himself from all conflicting elements of his personality and discovers the Divine within himself. So, too, within all other living beings and material objects, there is the centre of consciousness. He discovers the Divine in all things and in life.

In the Consciousness Approach, all items and problems of life are referred to the deepest inner consciousness which is the only centre of reference. Therefore, the Approach is applicable in so far as one places total reliance on the inner being because by the inner mastery it is possible to control all outer events. One must see the external industrial situations as the extension of his inner state of his consciousness expressed in outer life. The keys are really inside.

No attempt is made here to design a new system of management. Systems are mental. Our purpose is to evoke response in the business manager to the existence of a deeper centre of functioning in man and material from which all problems can be resolved in a higher order. The intention is the programme-evolution of the individual in general and a manager in particular towards solutions to life-problems with greater knowledge, care, love, power and beauty. The Consciousness Approach prescribes a process of 'Within-to-Without' management. This amounts to taking guidance from the Divine.

All can be done if the God-touch is there.[19]

The idea of strongest consequence at the base of Indian management, therefore, is the most dynamic inner spiritual life and approach. We live in an era where the springs of spiritual aspirations have not been dried by economic strangulation.

Quite possibly, all managers on the Indian scene may not find it possible to switch on, at one stroke, to the Consciousness Approach in their management process, because they are neck-deep in traditionalism, there is nothing to lose heart for the future because –

> Even if the struggling world is left outside,
> One man's perfection still can save the world.[20]

Let us aspire and make a beginning here and now. The question today is –

> The world is preparing for a big change.
> Will you help?[21]

Will you do your part?

DR. G. P. GUPTA

References:

1. Capra Fritjof: *The Turning Point* (1987), pp. 230-31.

2. Capra Fritjof: *The Impasse of Economics, The Turning Point* (1987), p. 243.

3. Sen, Indra: Lecture to Civil Servants at Simla (Quoted by K. R. Srinivasa Iyengar in The Yogic Approach to Management published in the Mother India, Sri Aurobindo Ashram, Pondicherry – 605002.

4. Sri Aurobindo: *Savitri* (Cent. Ed., Vol. 28), p. 169.

5. *Ibid.*, Book Two, Canto 5, p. 162.

6. *The Hour of God* (Cent. Ed., Vol. 17), p. 237.

6a. Sri Aurobindo: *Social and Political Thought* (Cent. Ed., Vol. 15), p. 105.

6b. Einstein A: *Out of My Later Years*, p. 260.

7. Sri Aurobindo: *Savitri* (Cent. Ed., Vol. 29), Book Eleven, Canto One, p. 705.

8. Sri Aurobindo: *Savitri* (Cent. Ed., Vol. 28), p. 20.

9. *Ibid.*, p. 32.

10. *Ibid.*, p. 186.

11. *Ibid.*, p. 49.

12. Sri Aurobindo: *Savitri* (Cent. Ed., Vol. 29), p. 448.

12a. *Ibid.*, Book Two Canto Six, p. 183.

13. *Ibid.*, Book Three Canto Two, p. 311.

14. *Ibid.*, Book Three SABCL. Vol. 28, p. 315.

15. *Ibid.*, p. 283.

16. *Ibid.*, Book One Canto Four, pp. 47-48.

17. *Ibid.*, p. 273.

18. *Ibid.*, p. 170.

19. Sri Aurobindo: *Savitri* (Cent. Ed., Vol. 29), p. 3.

20. *Ibid.*, p. 531.

21. *Collected Works of The Mother* (Cent. Ed. Vol. 15), p. 188.

11

THE MOTHER'S MINISTRY OF MANAGEMENT

Management is an exercise of harmonising men, material and methods towards fulfilment of goals leading to human development, social benefit and global welfare. However, MAN remains to be the basic factor in any field of human endeavour – may it be home, hospital, business, industry or any other profit/non-profit socio-economic organisation. By MAN we do not mean here only a 'lump' of bones and flesh, nor an 'amalgam' of hands, feet and other physical organism, not even a 'mental animal' contained in a physical frame, but a 'conscious creature' designed by the Divine Craftsman. He has a spirit and a soul. Management of man, therefore, should aim at not mere regulation and control of his outer appearance but it should also aim at developing his inner consciousness, his soul and his divinity.

In her scheme of management, the Mother of the Sri Aurobindo Ashram emphasised only the inner aspects of man and material and brought to develop the inner being for manifestation in the physical. In her management process, consciousness was her approach, harmony was her tool and perfection was her aim. Her approach to management was not sectoral or piecemeal, but experimental for the integral. Success was not her criterion, perfection was her goal. For outward manifestation she would develop the inner consciousness. For prosperity in living, life aspects should be prosperous, consciousness need be developed and the approach should be based on right attitude.

Faith and sincerity were the two pre-requisites of her management philosophy. Her organisational hierarchy was based on equality, trust, capacity and the nature of the individual. Centralisation of authority, if at all, was meant to diffuse and decentralise functions and power to perform them. Her ways were subtle, her base was spiritual and her approach was love. Fear was alien to her scheme of work and opening to the inner being was her impetus for the start.

With such traits of her management system, the Mother had managed the Ashram and its affiliates laying firm foundations for the welfare of posterity. Let us study some of these management processes to be emulated for our management policies and practice.

Central Authority

The Mother was the sole authority and all work could be done under Her authority and according to Her free decision. She was free to use the capacities of each separately or together according to what was best for the work and best for the worker.

One had to act under the Mother, carry out Her instructions, work according to ideas she had given him. She had laid down the lines on which he must work and whatever he does must be on those lines. He was not free to change them or to do anything contrary to the ideas given him. Where he makes decisions in details of the work, they must be in consonance with these lines and ideas. He has to report to the Mother, to take Her sanctions and accept Her decisions on all matters. If the Mother's decisions were contrary to his proposals he has still to accept them and carry them out.

The Mother had Her reasons for Her decisions. She had to look at work as a whole without regard to one department or branch alone and with a view to the necessities of the work and management. Whatever work was done, one had always to learn to subordinate or put aside one's own ideas and preferences about things concerning it and work for the best under the conditions and decisions laid down by Her.

Hierarchy

None could regard or treat another member of the Ashram as his subordinate. If he was in-charge, he could only regard the others as his associates and helpers in the work, and he should not try to dominate or impose on them his own ideas and personal fancies but only see to the execution of the will of the Mother. None could regard himself as a subordinate, even if he had to carry out instructions given through another or to execute under supervision the work he had to do.

All would try to work with harmony, thinking only of how best to make the work a success; personal feelings could not be allowed to interfere, for this was a most frequent cause of disturbance in the work, failure or disorder.

Let others be influenced by the rightness of your attitude and work smoothly with you, if through any weakness or perversity they create difficulties, the effect will fall back on them and you will feel no disturbance or trouble.

Decentralisation of Work

It was not physically possible for the Mother to allocate work directly to each worker and exercise a direct control. So for every department, therefore, there was to be a head who would consult Her in all important matters and would report everything to Her, but in minor matters he was autonomous and need not always come for a previous decision – and that was neither possible. But it did not mean that the Head of the Department was to be considered as a superior person or that he had to surrender to his ego. But those who had charge could insist on the execution of any arrangements.

It was the Mother who selected the heads of the departments for Her purpose in order to organise the whole. All the lines of the work, all the work had to be arranged by Her and the heads trained to observe Her methods and it was only afterwards that She stepped back and let the whole thing go on Her lines but with a watchful eye always. The Heads were to carry out Her policy and instructions and report everything to Her and she would often modify what they would do when She would think fit.

The head of a department was also supposed to act according to the Mother's directions – or in their spirit, when he was left free, and not otherwise. If he acted according to his mere fancy or obeyed his own personal likes and dislikes or misused his trust for his personal satisfactions or convenience he was answerable for any failure in the work that may result or wrong spirit or clash or confusion or false atmosphere.

The Mother did not usually think about things her-self, take the initiative and direct each one in each instance what they would do or how unless there was some special occasion for doing so. She would not do so, in fact, in any department of work. She would just keep Her eye generally on work, sanction or would correct or refuse sanction, intervene when she would think neces-sary. It was only a few matters in which she could take initiative, plan, design, give special and detailed orders. Work done in this way was as much work done accord-ing to the Mother's will as anything initiated, thought of and planned in whole and detail by Her alone.

Independent work does not exist in the Ashram. All is organised and inter-related – neither the heads of the departments nor the workers are independent. To learn subordination and co-operation was always necessary for all collective work; without it there could be chaos. It was impossible for the Mother to arrange the work according to personal considerations as then all work would become impossible.

Principle of Action

The Mother's principle of action was not to undertake useless and unnecessary work only in order to keep the men employed. She did not intervene at every moment to check persons at work. A standard had been set, they had been warned against waste, a framework had been created and for the rest they were expected to learn and grow out of their weaknesses by their own consciousness and will. In the organisation of work there was formerly a formidable waste due to workers following their own

fancy almost entirely without respect for Mother's will.
That was largely checked by reorganisation. But still the
waste continued. Here, too, the Mother did not always
insist. She watched and observed, intervened outwardly
more than in the individual lives of the sadhaks and still
left room for them to grow by consciousness and experience and the lessons of their own mistakes and often
employed an inner in preference to an outer pressure.

Material Responsibility

There were two foundations for the material life with
the Mother. The first was that one is a member of an
Ashram founded on the principle of self-giving and
surrender. One belongs to the Divine; in giving one
gives not what is one's own but what already belongs to
the Divine. There was thus no question of payment or
return, no bargain, no room for demand or desire. She
was under no obligation to act according to the mental
standards or vital desires and claims of the people; She
was not obliged to use a democratic equality in Her
dealings – She would deal with each according to his
true need or the best in his spiritual progress. Personal
demands and desires could not be imposed on Her. If
one was not ready to bear the discipline, he or she could
remain apart and meet his/her expenses. There was then
no discipline for him on the material plane and there
was no material responsibility for the Mother.

Consciousness Approach

The second foundation was the consciousness approach.

While dealing with men or material, She was very particular about this. She felt that physical things have a consciousness within them which feels and responds to care and is sensitive to careless touch and rough handling. To know or feel that and learn to be careful of them is a great progress of consciousness. It was always so that the Mother had felt and dealt with physical things and they remained with Her much longer and in a better condition than with others and give their full use.

The Mother believed in beauty as a part of spirituality and divine living. She believed that physical things have the Divine consciousness underlying them as much as living things. She believed that all physical things have an individuality of their own and ought to be properly treated, used in the right way, not misused or improperly handled or hurt or neglected so that they perish soon and lose their full beauty or value. She would feel the consciousness in them and was in so much sympathy with them that what in other hands may be spoilt or wasted in a short time would last with Her for years or decades.

Aesthetics and Orderliness

In management of material things, the Mother had a superb sense of aesthetic values. It was on this basis that She had planned the Golconde. First, she wanted a height of architectural beauty, and in this She succeeded – architects and people with architectural knowledge have admired it with enthusiasm as a remarkable achievement; one spoke of it as the finest building of its kind he had seen, with no equal in all Europe or

America; and a French architect, pupil of a great master, said it executed superbly the idea which his master had been seeking for but failed to realise. But the Mother also wanted all the objects in it, the rooms, the fittings, the furniture to be individually artistic and to form a harmonious whole. This, too, was done with great care. Moreover, each thing was arranged to have its own use, for each thing there was a place, and there could be no mixing up, or confused or wrong use. But all this had to be kept up and carried out in practice; for it was easy for people living there to create a complete confusion and misuse and to bring everything to disorder and ruination in a short time. That was why the rules were made. The Mother hoped that if right people were accommodated there or others trained to a less rough and ready living than is common, Her idea could be preserved and the wasting of all the labour and expense avoided.

Harmony

In the living patterns and behaviour of daily life, the Mother greatly emphasised upon harmony in man with man. The Mother believed that in relations with others, when incidents occur, it would be much better for one not to take the standpoint that he was all in the right and others were all in the wrong. It would be wiser to be fair and just in reflection, seeing where you have gone astray, and even laying stress on your own fault and not theirs. This leads to more harmony in your relations with others. At any rate, it would be more conducive to your inner progress which is more important than to be top-dog in a quarrel. Neither is it well to cherish a spirit of self-justification and self-righteousness and wish to conceal from yourself either your faults or your errors.

Where there was a big work with several people working together for a purpose which was not common to all and personal to any, it could not be done unless there was a fixed arrangement involving subordination and discipline in each worker. It would not be possible to get the work done if each and every worker insisted on being independent and directly responsible to the Mother or in doing things in his own way.

Mistakes come from people bringing their ego, their personal feeling (likes and dislikes) their sense of prestige of their convenience, pride, sense of possession into work. The right way was to feel that the work was not only yours, but the work of others and to carry it out in such a spirit that there shall be general harmony. Harmony cannot be brought about by external organisations only, though a more and more perfect organisation is necessary; inner harmony there must be or else there will always be clash and disorder.

Financial Management

About the financial arrangements: It was an arduous and trying work for the Mother to keep up the Ashram, with its ever-increasing numbers, to make both ends meet and at times to prevent deficit budgets and their results. Carrying on anything of this magnitude without any settled income could not have been done if there had not been the working of a Divine Force. The Mother started charging visitors for accommodation and food because she had expenses to meet but she charged in fact less than Her expense. The Mother never objected to people who "cannot pay" residing and visiting the Ashram without paying – she would expect payment only from visitors who could pay. She did really object strongly to the action of rich visitors who could pay, who had come, spent money lavishly on purchases etc. and went off without giving anything – that is all.

According to the Mother, money was not meant to bring more money – money was meant to increase the wealth, prosperity and the productiveness of a group, a country, or, preferably, the whole earth. As all forces and all powers, it is by activity and circulation that it grows and intensifies, not by accumulation and stagnation.

Waste

Free expenditure, according to the Mother, was not always waste. To have a higher standard than was current in the backward place was not necessarily a waste. In matters of building and maintenance of buildings as in others of the same order the Mother had from the very beginning set up a standard and she would not believe in the use of cheapest possible materials, the cheapest labour and to disregard appearance, allowing things to go shabbily or making only patch-work to keep them up.

If the higher standard was being kept, it was not for the glory of anyone – the Ashram, or the Mother – but from another point of view which was not mental but could only be fully appreciated by higher consciousness.

Austerity

The Mother did not provide the sadhaks with special comforts. She did not think that the desires, fancies, likings, preferences should be satisfied – in Yoga people had to overcome these things. The first rule of Yoga in the Ashram was that the sadhak must be content with what comes to him – much or little. If things are there, he must be able to use them without attachment or desire, if they were not, he must be indifferent to their absence.

Work

No work was high or low, according to the Mother. As for the work, the inner development, psychic and spiritual, was surely of the first importance and work merely as work was something quite minor. But work as an offering to the Divine becomes itself a means and a part of the inner development. That one can see more as the psychic grows within. It was not the work which was important, in the scheme of the Mother, but it was the spirit with which the work was done – that was all. The Mother has said – work through human body is the best prayer to the Divine, but that work must be done in the right spirit and with a right attitude.

Intimacy

The Mother always wanted to be very close and intimate with the sadhaks/workers to have a close communion with each of them on an inner plane. If She would ask you to tell Her everything, it was not in order that she might give you directions in every detail for your compliance. It was in order that there might grow up the complete intimacy in which you would be entirely open to Her, so that She might pour more and more and continuously and at every point the Divine Force into you and develop your nature. Besides, it would help Her to give whenever needed for necessary directions, the necessary help or warning – not always by words – more often by a silent intervention and pressure. This was Her way of dealing with those who were open to Her. Especially, if the psychic contact was there, it would get the intimation at once and see things clearly and receive the help, the necessary direction or warning.

Conclusion

To conclude, the Mother's ministry of management was based on the right attitude of man, his consciousness towards his inner being and his faith and sincerity to the Divine. The Mother was not a rigid disciplinarian. On the other hand, She had met the huge mass of indiscipline, disobedience, self-assertion, revolt that had surrounded Her, even revolt to Her very face and violent letters overwhelming Her with the worst kind of vituperation with constant leniency, tolerant patience and kindness. A rigid disciplinarian would not have treated things like that. It was only the Mother's authority, the frame of work she had given and Her skill in getting incompatibilities to act together that had kept things going. To quote the observation of a casual visitor:

Everywhere in the Ashram the visitor feels the atmosphere of an all-pervading executive genius.

Everything is done in the most perfect way. The combination of economy, efficiency, pleasantness and cleanliness is captivating. Nowhere is there any waste of substance. The blend of nature with engineering and art is exquisite and there is scarcely a building without its little garden of green grass, plants, foliage and enchanting flowers.

Mr. Eisenberg, the American expert on Management who had visited the Ashram said to himself – "Amazing experiment, most amazing experiment!"

India, says Sri Aurobindo, 'preserves the knowledge that preserves the world'. India has had a rich heritage and any management system, to be rich and enduring, must be based on this knowledge and Heritage.

Inaugurating a "Round-Table on India" organised by the Geneva-based European Management Forum in New Delhi, Shri Rajiv Gandhi, former Prime Minister of India, had asserted thus:

> The Indian mind is very receptive to quick changes, and we are able to absorb things much faster than many other people....
>
> We have to blend tradition with technology, not with Western materialism but with India's spiritualism.

This was what the Mother had preached and practised in the realm of management. Let us hope Her words shall endure!

DR. G. P. GUPTA

APPENDICES

APPENDICES

Appendix – I

YOGA IN MANAGEMENT

Yoga: Its Fundamentals

Man at his highest is a mental being. He perceives, knows, judges and wills action through the power of mind. Yoga begins when man awakens to an existence beyond, when he senses or feels a greater consciousness operative in the world, when he turns inwards and seeks to discover the Divine in himself, in the world or beyond this world. By this quest he grows in consciousness beyond the limitations of normal human nature and lives in a higher plane of existence with a more illumined knowledge, purer, vaster love and more powerful will for action. In his initial attempts to contact the Divine, man commonly resorts to prayer. Prayer is the linking of the human will with a higher power, the Divine will, for the fulfilment of a particular end, e.g. knowledge, love, happiness, health, wealth, strength, peace, etc. Prayer can issue from a thought in the mind, an emotion in the heart or from a deeper centre in man, the soul, which lies behind the heart and is in direct contact with the Divine. The power of prayer depends on its intensity as well as the sincerity and faith of the seeker. When these three elements are present in good measure, prayer is a far greater power for effectuation than any human endowment.

But prayer by its nature is an attempt to harness the Divine for one's own ends. At its highest prayer becomes an aspiration issuing from the soul not for any worldly end but for contact, identification and union with the Divine. At this point Yoga begins. Aspiration when it seeks to express itself in one's outer active life leads to consecration. Consecration literally means to make sacred. In Yoga this means doing an act as an offering to the Divine and with the Divine as the central reference. Instead of relying on and being moved by the normal human impulses, understanding and will, one seeks contact with the deep soul within and acts from that centre with its guidance. In effect, one suspends and offers one's own impulses, feelings, understanding and will-power so that a higher impulsion, truer knowledge and more powerful will can work through one. By this means the seeker gradually comes more in contact with the Divine and the Divine enters into and takes hold of his entire inner life and all his outer circumstances. Consecration leads to complete surrender and communion. Still a man acts in the world. When an act is fully consecrated it brings to bear a far greater power of consciousness than mind or prayers can generate.

The principles of management by consciousness are essentially a translation into mental terms for execution by the mental will of truths which are self-evident on higher planes of existence. Their power for effectuation depends on the development of the man's mind and the consecration of the will. In so far as one resorts to prayer or consecration, these methods grow in power beyond the human level and bring in the dynamism on the higher consciousness.

When an act is consecrated, it is no longer necessary to say that life responds to us. Rather it can be said that the Divine in life responds to the inner effort. The outer life becomes an expression of the inner consecration. Every outer obstacle and difficulty is an indication of the inner element to be worked upon and an inner progress to be made. When one exhausts all one's capacities and resources in consecrated activity, it is the higher power, the Divine Grace, that takes over. When one refuses to exercise human power of legal or moral right in deference to the Divine, the higher power enters through life and acts far more effectively than man. As the entire inner being is turned towards the Divine and opened to the higher consciousness, the outer life falls under control and all circumstances arrange themselves to aid in one's progress.

A Program for Business Management

Based on the practice of consecration a program has been developed, tested and proven very effective when applied to modern business institutions. The prerequisite for this program is for one to have established at least a minimum level of consecration in all his daily activities.

Consecration

1. Consecrate the physical body of the institution, i.e., the building, every room, the atmosphere. See all these as living things. Mentally recall that all these are manifestations of the Divine. Attempt to make an inner contact with them. Offer them to the service of the Divine. This can be made in one room each day.
2. Consecrate every piece of furniture, every object, and

every machine and the tool of work and production.

3. Consecrate the organisational hierarchy of the Organisation. Try to contact the deeper levels where all are One and in harmony. See the Divine at the top and within each position.

4. Consecrate every system and sub-system, e.g. telephone, mail, accounting, transportation, etc. Before work each morning consecrate these in advance. Then consecrate every call and piece of mail one attends to during the work day.

5. Consecrate every staff member, his personality's strengths and weaknesses, his professional skills, capabilities and limitations, his private life at home and his relations with staff and management, his interests, enthusiasms, fears and difficulties. This also means a consecration of your attitude, feelings, reactions towards the man. Try to establish a detached, disinterested objectivity toward his personality and an awareness of his true inner being.

6. Consecrate in detail the life history of the company – its founding ideals and emergence from previous types of institutions, its founder and builders, every past opportunity which was missed, every mistake, misdeed, misjudgement. Offer gratitude for every opportunity which came and for every progress as well as for every difficulty, when overcome, led to an advance. Look for a trend of strength which can be traced from the company's inception to the present. Look for a weakness which reappears periodically. Consecrate these strengths and weaknesses. Try to contact the inner being of the company, relate to it, identify with it, offer it to the service of the Divine.

7. Consecrate every new possibility for business, every new client and new sale. Offer gratitude.

8. Consecrate the role of money in the institution and every aspect of money exchange, that received and that paid out. Consecrate the company's policies, attitudes, practices in this regard.

9. See the next step which each element of the business should take in order to progress to a higher level. Consecrate those steps.

10. Consecrate every event and activity that occurs in your presence.

11. Enter into personal, silent, conscious relationship with every person, system, object and nourish them by your consciousness.

12. If any staff member takes up the consecration, the response will be greater.

Program of Activity

1. Study every employee silently to learn his talents and untapped potentials. Attempt to upgrade each employee to his maximum capacity.

2. Each employee should be conscious of what he contributes and what he receives. Relieve him of any false sense that he gives more than others and/or receives less recognition.

3. Note simple, avoidable sources of friction between employees and try to remove them by silent initiative.

4. Set all machinery in perfect, quiet working order.

5. Examine every system to see if it is working at maximum efficiency. Each system is a resource to be fully utilised.

6. See that all outer events such as mail, telephone call, obligations etc. are handled as quickly as possible. Work for maximum speed of response.

7. Work to increase cleanliness, orderliness, regularity, punctuality, peace, silence etc. even to a small extent.

8. Try to remove areas of secrecy, hiding etc., where falsehood prevails or which may encourage falsehood.

9. For every outer difficulty or problem, identify the corresponding inner point in the consciousness of management and staff.

10. If the atmosphere is receptive encourage management to initiate the study of the company including employee relations, use of machines and materials and operation of systems. Such a study should place emphasis on the possibilities for positive improvement and greater progress rather than on destructive criticism of others, self-defence or justification of the *status quo*.

Appendix – II

MANAGEMENT IS DEVELOPMENT OF MAN

> Whatever is the form of any arrangement or scheme, it has to be implemented by men. If the men continue to remain in darkness and falsehood, then no arrangement or scheme, however fine it may appear to be, can succeed.
>
> THE MOTHER

And it is best to begin with Man, the individual, because the society or nation, even in its greater complexity, is a larger, a composite individual – the collective Man. What we find valid of the former is likely to be valid in its general principle of the larger entity. Moreover, the development of the Man (free individual) is the first condition for the formation of a perfect society. From the Man, the individual – we must start, he should be our index and our foundation.

Man, as self, is a thing hidden and occult. It is not his body, it is not his life – even though he is in the scale of evolution the mental being – it is not his mind that makes a complete individual. Therefore, neither the fullness of his physical, nor of his vital, nor of his mental nature can be a true standard of his self-realisation.

The course of evolution proceeding from the vegetable to animal, from the animal to the man starts from the sub-human. He has to take into him the animal and even the mineral and vegetable. They constitute his physical nature, they dominate his vitality, they have their hold upon his mentality.

His readiness to vegetate, his proneness to many kinds of inertia, his blind servility to custom and the "rule of the pack", his mob-movements, his subjection to the yoke of rage and fear, his need and reliance on punishment, his inability to think and act for himself, his distrust of novelty, his subjection to his heredity – all these are his heritage from the sub-human origin of his life to body and physical mind. To learn by what he has been, and also to develop to what he can be, is the task that is set for modern "makers of mental beings".

Science, today, has prepared us for an age of wider and deeper culture – it has rendered impossible the return of the true materialism that of barbarian mentality. But it has encouraged more or less, both by attitude and discoveries, another kind of barbarism, that of the industrial, the commercial and the economic age. This economic barbarism is essentially that of the vital man who accepts its satisfaction as the first aim of life. The characteristic of this "Science Age" is desire and possession. Just as the physical barbarian makes the excellence of the body and physical force his standard and aim, so the economic barbarian makes the satisfaction of wants and desires and the accumulation of possessions his standard and aim. His ideal man is not the cultured or noble or thoughtful or moral or religious, but the successful man. To arrive, to succeed, to produce, to accumulate, to possess is his existence. The accumulation of wealth and more wealth, the adding of possessions to possessions, opulence, show, pleasure, a cumbrous inartistic luxury, a plethora of conveniences, life devoid of beauty and nobility, religion vulgarised or coldly formalised, politics and government turned into a trade and profession, enjoyment itself made a business, this is new commercialism. His idea of civilisation is comfort, his idea of morals social respectability, his idea of politics the encouragement of industry, the opening of markets, exploitation and 'trade following flag'. He values education, if at all, for its utility in filling a man for success in a socialised industrialised existence, science for the useful inventions, comforts and conveniences, machinery for power of production.

The opulent plutocrat and the successful mammoth capitalist and industrialist are the supermen of the commercial age and the true occult rulers of the society.

This vital part of the "modern man" is an element in the integral human existence as much as the physical part; it has its place but must not exceed its limits.

A full and well-appointed life is now desirable for man living in society, but on condition that it is a true and beautiful life. Therefore, in the modern commercial age, the soul may linger a while for some petty gains and experiences but could not permanently rest. If it persisted too long, life would become clogged and perish. Like the too massive Titan it will collapse by its own mass, *mole ruet sua*.

Hence, man must be chiselled to become a mental being, chastened and purified by a greater Law of Truth, good and beauty before he can take his proper place in the integrality of human perfection. Management must aim at developing an integrated man, a psychic man, a spiritual man and a perfect man and individual. Such an 'individual' alone will constitute a human factor of the Twenty-first century – a member of future society.

Appendix – III

MONEY: A DIVINE INSTRUMENT

In a creative economy of modern life, the role and importance of money cannot be overemphasised. Without money nothing can be achieved in material life. All socio-economic activities, all cultural gains and attainments, all creations and constructions (destructions), all trade, industry and commerce depend directly upon and are determined by money. Even the beggars and the lunatics recognise it and go asking for it. The ascetic has to depend upon money of others for his sustenance and his sermons. Money is a force, a lever of control and a power of possession. The index of modern (material) prosperity is money and money-power.

But money is not an unmixed blessing! It has brought in its train all deceits, defaults, evils, crimes, corruptions, demoralisations and degenerations. It is a source of much evil. But that is so with all material forces and powers in the world. One never thinks of eschewing fire because it burns, or water because it drowns. The human tendency is not to learn and act upon the advice and experiences of others – he craves to try experiments of his own. To be free from the vices of the world, we perhaps propose to shrink from the forces of life and do not gather courage to countenance them in their face. Instead of attempting and acquiring solutions of our ills we perhaps believe in a cowering retreat and not in conquest. But a total retreat is neither possible nor advisable. So long as the body is there, a shunning attitude is not advisable nor is it possible to eliminate the detestables. For that reason, perhaps, an ascetic is compelled to compromise with the forces he despises and dreads and yet cannot overcome and avoid.

The real solution to ills of money that it brings in its train lies in understanding it through the mechanism of Divinity. If the human life, as such, has to be reorganised on the basis of Divine Consciousness, the money power, too, will have to be looked upon as an 'Instrument of the Divine'. If we fight shy of it, our progress will remain poor, halting and choked. To really understand the meaning of money as a lever of rich and powerful creative material life in the world, we will have to redefine the contents and the conditions of money as a medium of social good and human progress. According to Sri Aurobindo:

> Money is the visible sign of a universal force, and this force in its manifestation on earth works on the vital and physical planes and is indispensable to the fullness of the outer life. In its origin and its true action it belongs to the Divine. But like other powers of the Divine it is delegated here and in the ignorance of the lower Nature can be usurped for the uses of the ego or held by Asuric influences and perverted to their purpose. This is indeed one of the three forces – power, wealth, sex – that have the strongest attraction for the human ego and the Asura and are most generally misheld and misused by those who retain them. The seekers or keepers of wealth are more often possessed rather than its possessors; few escape entirely a certain distorting influence stamped on it by its long seizure and

perversion by the Asura.

Thus, money is a universal force derived, like other forces from the Divine. But, like every other force, it is appropriated and perverted by the beings of darkness and is used to serve and satisfy their own ends.

Well, we plan to set up a Divine life on earth and for that reason alone the divine use of money will have to be our first imperative. 'The aversion against money or feel against its misuse will be our timidity, truancy from reality, anaemic spirituality and flight from our ancient ideality'. Let us understand that all wealth, all splendour, all significance emerge from the Divine, and if matter is for the Divine, then material wealth is also from the Divine. Sri Aurobindo holds that it is usurped here in the material world "for the uses of the ego held by Asuric influences and perverted to their purpose."

Thus money is a product of the Divine, an instrument of setting up Life Divine on earth – the need is that it has to be extricated from the hold of the Asuras and used for the service of the Divine in the world. Money cannot be dispensed with. For a harmonious progressive and luminous life on earth money, like all material means, is indispensable and none should plead for its extinction from earthly life.

The real danger, however, is that most of the present possessors of money have become possessed by money-power. Instead of their being masters of money, they have become slaves of money-power and are governed by the vital forces like desires – say for food, fame and furnishings. Money is watered down for the baser needs and this lavishness is not only justified, but admired as a large-hearted munificence. The society praises such selfish use of money and expects that the right/wrong uses of money can be analysed only through the motives, attitude and the consciousness of the possessor.

A moneyed man plans to spend a lakh of rupees for his son's marriage. He imbibes this idea either by force of all social customs or traditions or conceives it independently through an impulse arising in or invading him. Therefore, the rich man submits to vital forces operating in his society or succumbs unawares to their fresh assaults upon him. In either case, it is not the decision of his true self; but those forces that profit by and enjoy by this enormous expenditure. This enjoyment and pleasure derived from the huge expenditure is exclusively a vital pleasure, which obscures his consciousness, satisfies his pride and ego and retards his spiritual evolution. Says the Mother:

> The vital power controlling money is like a guardian who keeps his wealth in a big safe always tightly closed. Each time the people who are in its grasp are asked to part with their money, they put all sorts of careful questions before they will consent to open their purses even a very little way; but if a vital impulse arises in them with its demands, the guardian is happy to open wide the coffer and money flows out freely.

This leads to assert that in 90% of the cases we make use of money in an illegitimate and unspiritual way, which degrades our consciousness and prompts us to put a ban on money. Not only do we lose much of the money we use, but we lose into the bargain the precious opportunities for using it for the service of the Divine to whom it really belongs. Says Sri Aurobindo:

> All wealth belongs to the Divine and those who hold it are trustees, not possessors. It is with them today, tomorrow it may be elsewhere. All depends on the way they discharge their trust while it is with them, in what spirit, with what consciousness in their use of it, to what purpose.

The proper use of money is to win it from the hands of the vital forces and then to divert it into the developing channels of the Divine Work. But one must remember here that the acts of altruism or philanthrophy are not, as is commonly understood, selfless or disinterested. We do them because the ego in us takes a positive delight in them – a self-regarding delight, full of pride and complacency. "In your personal use of money look on all you have or get or bring as the Mother's... Be entirely selfless, entirely scrupulous, exact, careful in detail, a good trustee; always consider that it is in her possessions and not your own that you are handling." Think that the material life and its powers and resources have been given to us not for the egoistic satisfaction of our desires and cravings but for the realisation of the Divine Will and its perfect fulfilment. Then alone it will loose and finally abolish the ego's grip upon us in our use of money. The degrading bondage of money has to be annulled, not by flight from it, but by a complete conquest over it. It is not enough to be unegoistic and disinterested in our use of money, we have to be powerful instruments of the Divine which alone will guide us to use the money-power for establishing Life Divine on earth.

No dynamic spirituality can afford to put a ban on money, for that will mean leaving the money-power in the hands of the vital forces on the one hand and on the other paralysing material world by poverty. Like other powers it has to be reconquered for the Divine to be used divinely for the Divine purpose in human life. In the beginning, it will be difficult for one to know for certain what the service of the Divine is. His ego may wear various disguises and delude him into wrong decisions. Very few people have the capacity to detect the ego in the acts of selflessness because the ego's hold is stronger for altruistic and philanthropic activities. But if a man clearly feels that he belongs to the Divine and all that he has also belongs to the Divine then the ego's dominance begins to diminish and the centre of consciousness opens in him to give him the right lead in his use of money. Little by little, a clear perception and a definite direction of the will takes the place of doubts and uncertainties and things become easy and natural. Later, by further verification of our nature and consciousness another centre opens up high above and gives an infallible lead to the movements of our being. This is the way to deal with money so far as we are individually concerned with it.

COMMERCIALISM AND ECONOMIC UNITY

Commercialism is a modern sociological phenomenon – that is the whole phenomenon of modern society. The economic part of life is always important to an organised community and even fundamental.

In former times it was simply the first need, it was that which occupied the thoughts of men, gave the whole tone to the social life, stood at the helm and was clearly recognised as standing at the root of social principles. Sri Aurobindo has claimed that "The economic impulses of the group were worked out as a mechanical necessity, a strong desire in the vital being rather than a leading thought in the mind." "Ancient man was in the group primarily a political being, in the Aristotelian sense... and to this preoccupation he added, wherever he was sufficiently at ease, the preoccupation of thought, art and culture."[1]

Nor was the society regarded or studied as an economic organism except in a very superficial aspect. The economic man had an honourable, but still a comparatively low position in the society – he was only the third caste/class – the *Vaishya*. The lead was in the hands of the intellectual and political classes – the *Brahmin*, thinker, scholar, philosopher and priest; the *Kshatriya*, ruler and warrior. It was their thoughts and pre-occupations that gave the tone to society, determined its conscious drift and action, coloured most powerfully all its motives. Commercial interests did enter into the relations of States and into the motives of war and peace; but their role was secondary and subordinate to be only causes of strife, alliance and peace. The political motive and consciousness had dominated; increase of wealth was primarily regarded as a means of political power and greatness and opulence of economic resources of the state than as an end in itself or a first consideration.

Now, everything is changed. At present, it is the *Vaishya* who predominates and his stamp on the world is commercialism – the predominance of the economic man, the universality of the commercial value for everything and the materially efficient and productive human life. Even in the outlook on knowledge, thought, science, art, poetry and religion the economic conception of life overrides all the rest.

II

For the modern economic view of life, culture has retained only a decorative value – it is a costly luxury and not at all an indispensable necessity. Religion remains to be a by-product of the human mind with a very restricted utility, if at all. Education does have a recognised importance but no longer cultural, scientific and utilitarian but merely as a tool to preparing an efficient individual unit to take his place in the body of economic organisation. Science is, of course, of an immense importance but not because it discovers the secrets of Nature for the advancement of knowledge, but only because it utilises them for the creation of machinery and develops and organises the economic resources of the community. Politics, government are becoming more and more a machinery for the development of an industrialised society and to serve Economic Socialism. Free thought remains to be on the surface of this great increasing mass of commercialism to influence or modify it, but is itself influenced, penetrated, coloured and subjugated by the economic, commercial and industrial view of human life. The economic order, as it is, is not equitable and does not do justice to us.

This fundamental change has affected profoundly the character of international relations and is likely to affect them still more openly and powerfully in the future. Certain prophetic voices announce indeed the speedy passing of the age of modern commercialism. But it is not easy to see how this is to come about. Surely, it will not be by a reversion to the predominantly political spirit of the past or the temper and forms of the old aristocratic social life. The end of modern commercialism can only come about either by some unexpected development of new-commercialism or through a re-awakening of spirituality in the race and its coming to its own by the subordination of the political and economic motives of life to the spiritual motives. Let us quote here the prophetic pronouncement of Sri Aurobindo:

> ...for when material circumstances favour a great change, but the heart and mind of the race are not really ready – especially the heart – failure may be predicted, unless indeed men are wise in time and accept the inner change alongwith the external re-adjustment.[2]

III

However, certain signs seem to be taking form in this direction. The religious spirit is reviving and even the old discouraged religions, creeds and forms are regaining a kind of vigour. In the secular thought of mankind there are signs of an idealism assuming a spiritual element among its motives. But all this is as yet slight and superficial. The impulsion is still towards the industrialising of the human race and the perfection of social life as an economic and productive organism. It is aided still by modern socialism which promises to be the master of the future. It intends indeed to substitute Labour as the Master instead of Capital. This reflects that all activities will be valued by the labour contributed and work produced rather than by the wealth contribution and production. It will be a change from one brand of economism to the other, but not a change from economism to the higher motive of human life.

IV

In the past, the effect of commercialism had been to bind together the human race into a real economic unity despite its political separativeness. But because the organised units were politically separate and rival nations, their commercial inter-relations became cause of conflicts and rivalry. Obviously, the results were: self-defence by tariff walls, race for closed markets, exploitation, struggle for predominance and monopolisation of markets and inter-penetration in spite of tariff-walls resulting into mutual hostility and separativeness. The outbreak of war under such conditions remains only to be a matter of moments. The shock of war is rendered intolerable by the industrial organisation of human life and the commercial inter-dependence of the nations. From this point of view, the prevention of war must be one of the first pre-occupations of a new ordering of international life. But how is war to be entirely prevented if a state of commercial rivalry between politically separate nations has been perpetuated?

Let us suppose that the physical shock of war be prevented, not by Law, but by enforced arbitration; by creation of international authority or by the overhanging threat of international pressure. But as examples are, the state of covert war will still continue and it may take new and disastrous forms. Deprived of other weapons the nations may have increasing resort to the weapon of commercial pressures – economic sanctions, commercial boycott, refusal of capital and machinery, prohibition of all or needed imports, naval blockade and even restrictive trade policies and practices.

V

But so long as there is not a firm World Authority the use of such weapons would not be made for just and legitimate ends. These might be used by a strong nation to crush and violate the weak; these might also be used by a combination of strong powers to enforce their selfish and evil will upon the world. Force and coercion of any kind not concentrated in the hands of a just and impartial authority are always liable to be misused. Therefore, inevitably in the growing unity of mankind the formation of a World Authority also does not seem to be a sound solution. Let us heed in this connection to a word of caution from Sri Aurobindo:

> It is therefore quite improbable that in the present conditions of the race a healthy unity of mankind can be brought about by State machinery... Such an external or administrative unity may be intended in the near future of mankind in order to accustom the race to the idea of a common life, to its habit, to its possibility; but it cannot be really healthy, durable or beneficial over all the true line of human destiny unless something be developed, more profound, internal and real... The experiment will break down and give place to a new reconstructive age of confusion and anarchy... it ought to be possible for us now to avoid it by subordinating mechanical means to our true development through a moralised and even a spiritualised humanity united in its inner soul and not only in its outward life and body.[3]

References:

1. Social and Political Thought: *The Ideal of Humanity* (Cent. Ed., Vol. 15), p. 463.
2. *Ibid:*, p. 263.
3. *Ibid.*, p. 284.

Appendix – V

MATERIALISM AND SPIRITUALITY

The West and the East

...it has been customary to dwell on the division and difference between these two sections of the human family and even oppose them to each other; but, for myself I would rather be disposed to dwell on oneness and unity than on division and difference. East and West have the same human nature, a common human destiny, the same aspiration after a greater perfection, the same seeking after something higher than itself, something towards which inwardly and even outwardly we move. There has been a tendency in some minds to dwell on the spirituality or mysticism of the East and the materialism of the West; but the West has had no less than the East its spiritual seekings and, though not in such profusion, its saints and sages and mystics, the East has had its materialistic tendencies, its material splendours, its similar or identical dealings with life and Matter and the world in which we live. East and West have always met and mixed more or less closely, they have powerfully influenced each other and at the present day are under an increasing compulsion of Nature and Fate to do so more than ever before.

There is a common hope, a common destiny, both spiritual and material, for which both are needed as co-workers. It is no longer towards division and difference that we should turn our minds, but on unity, union, even oneness necessary for the pursuit and realisation of

a common ideal, the destined goal, the fulfilment towards which Nature in her beginning obscurely set out
and must in an increasing light of knowledge replacing
her first ignorance constantly persevere.

But what shall be that ideal and that goal? That
depends on our conception of the realities of life and the
supreme Reality.

Here we have to take into account that there has been,
not any absolute difference but an increasing divergence
between the tendencies of the East and the West. The
highest truth is truth of the Spirit; a Spirit supreme
above the world and yet immanent in the world and in
all that exists, sustaining and leading all towards whatever is the aim and goal and the fulfilment of Nature
since her obscure inconscient beginnings through the
growth of consciousness is the one aspect of existence
which gives a clue to the secret of our being and a
meaning to the world. The East has always and increasingly put the highest emphasis on the supreme
truth of the Spirit; it has, even in its extreme philosophies, put the world away as an illusion and regarded
the Spirit as the sole reality. The West has concentrated
more and more increasingly on the world, on the
dealings of mind and life with our material existence, on
our mastery over it, on the perfection of mind and life
and some fulfilment of the human being here: latterly
this has gone so far as the denial of the Spirit and even
the enthronement of Matter as the sole reality. Spiritual
perfection as the sole ideal on one side, on the other, the
perfectibility of the race, the perfect society, a perfect
development of the human mind and life and man's
material existence have become the largest dream of the

future. Yet both are truths and can be regarded as part of the intention of the Spirit in world-nature; they are not incompatible with each other: rather their divergence has to be healed and both have to be included and reconciled in our view of the future.

The Science of the West has discovered evolution as the secret of life and its process in this material world; but it has laid more stress on the growth of form and species than on the growth of consciousness: even, consciousness has been regarded as an incident and not the whole secret of the meaning of the evolution. An evolution has been admitted by certain minds in the East, certain philosophies and Scriptures, but there its sense has been the growth of the soul through developing or successive forms and many lives of the individual to its own highest reality. For if there is a conscious being in the form, that being can hardly be a temporary phenomenon of consciousness; it must be a soul fulfilling itself and this fulfilment can only take place if there is a return of the soul to earth in many successive lives, in many successive bodies.

The process of evolution has been the development from and in inconscient Matter of a subconscient and then a conscious Life, of conscious mind first in animal life and then fully in conscious and thinking man, the highest present achievement of evolutionary Nature. The achievement of mental being is at present her highest and tends to be regarded as her final work; but it is possible to conceive a still further step of the evolution: Nature may have in view beyond the imperfect mind of man a consciousness that passes out of the mind's ignorance and possesses truth as its inherent right and nature. There is a Truth-Consciousness as it is called in the Veda, a Supermind, as I have termed it, possessing knowledge, not having to seek after it and constantly miss it. In one of the Upanishads a being of knowledge is stated to be the next step above the mental being; into that the soul has to rise and through it to attain the perfect bliss of spiritual existence. If that could be achieved as the next evolutionary step of Nature here, then she would be fulfilled and we could conceive of the perfection of life even here, its attainment of a full spiritual living even in this body or it may be in a perfected body. We could even speak of a divine life on earth; our human dream of perfectibility would be accomplished and at the same time the aspiration to a heaven on earth common to several religions and spiritual seers and thinkers.

The ascent of the human soul to the supreme Spirit is that soul's highest aim and necessity, for that is the supreme reality; but there can be too the descent of the Spirit and its powers into the world and that would justify the existence of the material world also, give a meaning, a divine purpose to the creation and solve its riddle. East and West could be reconciled in the pursuit of the highest and largest ideal, Spirit embrace Matter and Matter find its own true reality and the hidden Reality in all things in the Spirit.

SRI AUROBINDO

ABOUT THE CONTRIBUTORS

WESTON H. AGOR — Professor and Director of the Master in Public Administration Program at the University of Texas at El Paso (Texas) USA – Also a Consultant on the use of intuition in Management for several American Organisations including Walt Disney Enterprises and Rockwell International.

K.R. SRINIVASA IYENGAR — Formerly Professor of English in several universities in India – Sometime visiting Professor of Indo-Anglian Literature, University of Leeds, the U.K. – Vice-Chancellor of Andhra University – President, Sahitya Academy – Renowned thinker and Interpreter of Indian Literature, Culture and Fine Arts – Prolific Writer on Literature, Education, Mysticism and allied problems of life and living – an ardent devotee of Sri Aurobindo and the Mother – Member of the Executive Committee of Sri Aurobindo Society, Pondicherry.

GARY JACOBS — Writer and Consultant on problems of Business Management based on Consciousness Approach of Sri Aurobindo. One time stayed in Sri Aurobindo Ashram, Pondicherry and studied intensively the Consciousness Approach of Sri Aurobindo and The Mother.

G.P. GUPTA — Formerly Professor, Chairman, Dean and Director, Schools of Business Management and Commerce in Indian Universities – Visiting Faculty to Universities in the USA – Lectured on Contemporary Problems of Management in Japan, the USA, the UK, Germany and other West European countries – Coordinator of non-traditional Management-oriented courses at Birlagram, Nagda (M.P.) – currently Honorary Director of S.C. Institute of Management Education and Research, Pondicherry.

SWAMI RANGANATHANANDA — Senior monk of the Ramakrishna Order – Trustee of the Ramakrishna Math,
and a member of the Governing Body of the Ramakrishna Mission – One of the most respected and
loved eminent scholars of the country discoursing
inter alia on the Gita, the Upanishads, the Vedanta
and other subjects relating to man's spiritual quest
and human development – widely travelled speaker
on cultural and spiritual topics.

INDEX